TOUGH CALLS

Tough Calls

Selling Strategies to Win Over Your Most Difficult Customers

Josh Gordon

American Management Association

New York • Atlanta • Boston • Chicago • Kansas City • San Francisco • Washington, D.C.
Brussels • Mexico City • Tokyo • Toronto

Library of Congress Cataloging-in-Publication Data

Gordon, Josh.
    Tough calls : selling strategies to win over your most difficult
customers / Josh Gordon.
      p. cm.
    Includes index.
    ISBN 0-8144-7925-1
    1. Selling. I. Title.
HF5438.25.G665   1996
658.85—DC20   96-35064
                                             CIP

Printing number

10 9 8 7 6 5 4

For **Lynn** on our tenth
For **Laura** on her sixth
For **Jenny** on her second

Contents

TOUGH CALLS

Introduction:
Why Another Book
on Selling?

Traditional selling techniques—and the books that cover them—work well when clients behave themselves and play fair. But most often, problem clients cannot be sold through conventional approaches. The national survey I conducted to write this book found that, on average, one out of every six clients is a problem client. *Tough Calls* is the first book written that will give you specific strategies on how to SELL them.

Many proven selling approaches that work well with most clients can backfire when used in a problem client situation. For example, using a trial close to flush out objections before going for a final close works well with most clients. But using it with a client who is an egomaniac can backfire. Egomaniacs most always have to be right all of the time, and if they say "no" to you in a trial close, it is sometimes much harder to get them to say "yes" later on.

At some client companies, "getting tough" with suppliers to get better prices or concessions is encouraged from the very top, and intimidating salespeople who come to call is considered to be behaving in an appropriate manner. At other companies where "reorganization" is in the wind, many clients are just too insecure to make sound buying decisions, which results in problematic behavior. Some companies put people with difficult personalities or little talent into buying positions. They might say, "We can't fire him, and he will do little big-picture damage there." Then there are the problem clients who do not fit the "problem people" model. They may be extremely professional, but like a competitor's product better than yours, buy on established relationships, or be tied up with company politics. This book will help you cope with all of these and other problem client selling situations in specific terms.

How the Book Is Set Up

Through research I have identified twenty problem client behaviors that account for the vast majority of problem client behavior you will ever encounter and each one has a chapter in this book dedicated to it. Each chapter contains strategies on how to spot a problem client while you can still make a difference; "Pitfalls," or what you should avoid with a particular problem client; "Selling Strategies," which give you specific ideas on how to persuade the client to buy; and "Closing Strategies," which give you specifics on how to close that particular problem client.

I do not present any "best" or "only" way to sell or close any of these problem clients, rather I present a collection of the best ideas. My intention is for you to be able to pick and choose among them and find a solution that fits your selling style and your particular client. In some chapters I present selling strategies that conflict with one another, and in other chapters I present strategies that I have seen other salespeople use successfully that I do not use or recommend. You choose the approach that will work for you.

I end *Tough Calls* with an overview chapter that presents research findings from The Tough Calls Survey, a national survey I conducted for this book. I used three separate mailing lists and sent out close to one thousand questionnaires. By comparing your personal problem client experiences with the national averages, you can come away with a better understanding of how you are doing.

Why *Tough Calls* Is the Opposite of Most Books on Selling

If you haven't noticed, most books on selling (including one I wrote five years ago) concern the behavior of salespeople (giving presentations, closing, answering objections, etc.). *Tough Calls* does the opposite; it focuses on the behavior of your clients first and recommends selling approaches directed toward that behavior.

Writing about the selling process from this opposite point of view gave me the opportunity to describe selling approaches that have not been written about before. For example, how do you get an egomaniac to think your idea to buy was his? See Chapter 17.

Why Another "Problem People" Book?

Problem clients present a fundamentally different challenge than other kinds of problem people for two big reasons.

1. As salespeople and people in client contact situations our job is to SELL clients, not just cope with them.
2. In the buyer-seller relationship, problematic behavior is most often designed to get a result. Very little problem client behavior is the result of a regrettable problem personality. The national survey conducted for this book found that only about 10 percent of problem clients act the way they do because they have a problem personality. Most problem client behavior is motivated behavior, designed to get a result. As a salesperson your job is to recognize problem client behavior early, get around it or use it to your advantage, and move on to close a sale. Taking a "business as usual" approach can be disastrous.

Finally, please consider that every one of your current clients has the potential to become a problem client (see Chapter 9, "The Client Who May Cancel the Order"), and many of your good clients will show signs of these problematic behaviors at some time during your relationship with them.

It's tough out there! Good reading!

1

The Client Who
Grinds You on Price

From the Tough Calls survey:

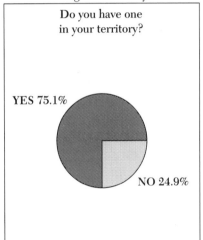

Do you have one
in your territory?

YES 75.1%

NO 24.9%

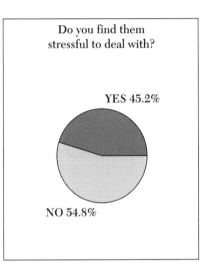

Do you find them
stressful to deal with?

YES 45.2%

NO 54.8%

"It is an excuse that is the easiest to use."

Industrial Goods Salesman, Dallas, Texas

The Price Grinder will relentlessly try to get you to lower your price. He may tell you he doesn't need your product and that he can get the same for less from your competitor. He may tell you what other competitors are doing in terms of price and that if you don't lower your price he will give his business to them.

Usually you can see the Price Grinder coming. When an associate of mine made an appointment to visit a Price Grinder, she was told, "I'll be looking forward to our visit, Ann Belle, but just remember to bring your sharpest pencil." When I asked a Price Grinder for an appointment at a trade show, he said, "Before I agree, I want to see a rate card." I handed him one, and without even looking at it, he tore it up in little pieces and threw it on the ground in front of me. "That's what I think of rate cards," he sneered. "Do you still want the appointment?"

Price Grinders can pop up in surprising places. My least favorite Price Grinder is the one who ambushes you. He leads you into thinking he is an extremely legitimate client with lots of potential. Then, as you are salivating, seconds away from closing a big sale that will lead to more big sales, he hits you with a big scene about your outrageous prices. If you feel that a client is selling you on how important he is to your business, you may be getting set up for an ambush. Never forget who is supposed to be selling whom.

Pitfalls

1. Getting so focused on price that you forget to sell your product.

Selling is not about giving the lowest price; it's about offering the best value. Even if your client pretends not to pay attention, it's important to find a way to sell the value of your product. If it seems that price is all he cares about, use that as the hook to make your points: "I know you want to talk about the bottom line, so I want you to be clear on the elements that make up my product so that you can understand our pricing." Then go into a description of your product value. If all you are is the lowest cost provider, your customer will be gone the next time a lower-priced vendor shows up.

2. Discussing price first.

The time to sell the value of your product is before price comes up. The temptation is to talk about price first since that is what the Price Grinder will tell you is all he cares about. But as soon as price comes up, the tone and psychology of the sales call change. After demands for pricing concessions are made, everything that comes afterward seems like defensive selling to justify a price, rather than an honest effort to explain real benefits. To effectively sell the Price Grinder, you must talk about the value of your product first.

3. *Wasting your time on Price Grinders who are not serious customers.*

There really are clients who are so focused on price that they cannot be sold. For them price is everything, even if it's just two dollars off a thousand-dollar order. Get a price concession of any kind, offer it to them, and see whether they will buy. If they don't, move on and spend your time on a client with whom you really can make a difference.

Ultimately many Price Grinders are not worth doing business with. They can represent an unprofitable company that will drain you and your organization of energy and time, with more demands than the business they send you is worth. Also, it can be a very short-term benefit if you do sell them. If every nickel they spend is so dear that they have a major fight over it, cash flow may be very unstable at that company. If, on the other hand, you are working in an industry where your client's customers relentlessly demand low prices, get used to dealing with Price Grinders. They may be the long-term players in your industry.

4. *Believing what a Price Grinder tells you about your competitors' pricing.*

While selling for Harvey Research, Paul Cohen offered a research service to a client who told him that he could buy a product similar to the one he was selling for $3,000. Now, Paul knew this could not be true and, knowing the pricing components of the research study he was selling, began to ask his client some questions: "So you are telling me that this competitor will mail 700 questionnaires with a dollar incentive in each one." The client agreed. "OK, that will cost $700." Paul wrote $700 on a yellow pad. "Now you've told me that he will also mail out 700 copies of your magazine along with this mailing." The client agreed. Paul said, "OK, that will cost another $1,750." Paul wrote this number on his yellow pad. By the time Paul had accounted for every element of the service his competitor had allegedly offered, it was clear that the service was being offered at a money-losing price. Paul explained why his service was better, didn't budge on price, and left the office. A month later the client called him back to begin using Paul's service. Said Paul, "Sometimes these clients just give you a line, like 'Your competitor is giving it to me at 70 percent off.' Maybe they are getting a discount, maybe it's 30 to 40 percent off, but not what they tell you it is."

5. Underestimating him and thinking he's just a crazy pain in the neck.

True Price Grinders are master craftsmen who have honed their skills over the years. If they spent more time running a better business and less time working to get lower prices on everything, the company they work for would be far better off. But for the Price Grinder, the sport of getting the lowest price can be more important than buying the best product at a fair price. You may say he is crazy and doing his company damage, but often the Price Grinder is "crazy like a fox" and does end up getting what he wants. More often the person driven crazy is you.

Selling Strategies

1. When you are asked for a price concession, ask for something in return.

This is the quickest way to separate the serious rate negotiator from the "it doesn't hurt to ask" negotiator. Tell him he can have his price but he must give you more business (or something else you want). If your client is not so serious about a rate demand, then you have effectively said no by putting the ball back in his court. If he is serious, he will get back to you. For example:

> **Client:** We need you to lower your system price by another 10 percent or we will give the bid to a competing firm.

Salesperson:	We will lower our price by 10 percent, but you will have to guarantee us a 20 percent increase in business over the next year.
Client:	A 20 percent increase in business? We could increase business a little bit but not by 20 percent. As the proposal stands you are getting our entire capital budget for the year.
Salesperson:	OK, what if we lower our price by 5 percent and you sign up for our after-sale service program? That wouldn't come out of a capital budget, and you are going to have to sign a service contract with someone.
Client:	We would like to get a 5 percent discount. Let's look at the numbers for the service contract. If you can offer us a price comparable to what we are getting from our current supplier, you have a deal.

By asking for something in return, you will see just how much value is placed on the demand for a price concession. Here by asking for something in return, at first a 20 percent increase in business, the salesperson uncovered just how serious the client's demand was: not nearly as significant as it was made to appear at first ("or we will give the bid to a competing firm"), but significant enough to warrant shifting a service contract from another supplier to ensure a discount.

This kind of give-and-take exchange usually scares off the phony demands, and if you do end up giving a concession it will not be viewed as a sign of weakness.

2. Remember, every Price Grinder has a boss.

Often when a client really grinds you on price, it's to make himself look good in front of his boss. In business-to-business selling, unlike consumer selling, most often the customer *has* the money to buy the product you are selling. But he wants to look good. If he gets a price out of you, then he goes back to his boss and gets a raise. The way you can keep from getting ground on price is to give the client you are calling on reasons to present to his boss to justify the price.

I was once put under tremendous price pressure while selling ad space to an ad agency. The agency was, in effect, acting as the purchasing agent for the client. Once I got to the client directly and made him believe he had to buy space in my magazine, the agency's demand for price concessions disappeared. Sometimes if the ultimate client is sold, the purchasing agents will grind price somewhere else.

3. Keep it personal.

With price negotiation, less personal negotiations will favor the buyer. It is much easier to gouge or make crazy price demands of someone you don't know very well. If you have had dinner with the client, chances are you will be treated at the very least fairly. For example, suppose my client comes home to his wife and tells her I visited him that day:

> **Client:**   Honey, remember Josh Gordon, that space rep for Government Data Systems? Well, he came to see me today.
>
> **Wife:**   Yes, dear, he was the one who took us out to that wonderful French restaurant. I still remember it. He ordered that nice bottle of wine and an extra dessert to bring home for the kids . . . it was just perfect. Such a nice person. His wife was pregnant, wasn't she? Well what did he have to say?. . .

Imagine how my client would respond to this, if he had really beaten me senseless over rates?

Russ Thibeault of the Intertec Electrical Group had to negotiate every year with one particular Price Grinder. When the call came in for another round, Russ would let the call go unreturned for a day, just to let the emotion drain out of it. Then Russ would proceed as follows: "When I got on the phone I would acknowledge where he was coming from. I would listen to his side and work toward getting some kind of agreement with him. 'OK, your client is coming under increased price pressure, and that is being passed on to you, and you are passing this on to me.' OK. Then I would let him know that we were in this together. He had to look good in front of his client but he had to understand that I had to look good in front of my boss. Together we would work slowly toward an agreement where both sides could give up a little, but no one side came off as major loser. This avoided a major head-slamming confrontation where everyone lost."

4. Find out what your client really wants.

A price demand means many different things to many different clients. For some it really is a straight request for paying less cash. However, I find this to be true in only a minority of cases. A request for lower prices is more often a request for one of the following:

- A way to look good before a superior by squeezing some extra blood out of you. If there are other ways you can make him look like a hero, cave in there and leave your pricing intact.
- A win. They win, you lose, they buy. Some Price Grinders just feel that they have not done their job until they have seen you sweat. Is there some other area in which they can win where they will still buy?
- Ego gratification. Often rate negotiation really is an ego issue for the client. Some clients just want the satisfaction of knowing that they got something extra. If this is the case, give them something extra that does not involve cutting rates.
- A need to be sold further on the value of your product. A price is too high when it exceeds the perceived value of the product being sold. But if the client perceives that the product is worth more, then is the price still too high?

See whether you can give a concession in a place other than price. If you can discover the deeper needs of the client you are negotiating with, you will have more horses to trade when the horse trading begins.

5. *Sell value.*

You must turn the discussion around. Instead of listening to the Price Grinder justify why your product isn't worth its price, you have to sell him on why it is. Say, "OK, let's put price aside. Tell me what you are looking for in a (whatever)." Once the client tells you, you can begin to match your product up to his needs. When you find you have a good match ask, "So what are we talking about in terms of a price difference, $200?" Once you get price off the table you will find out what the real objection is. Usually it's not about price.

6. *Differentiate your product from that of your competitors.*

Before you can prove that your product is better, you have to prove that it is different. If your client can't see the difference between the products you are competing with, then he should buy the cheapest one. If you let him win the argument that your product is a commodity, then price is the only differentiating factor. Don't accept his view that your product is a commodity.

Even if the products are nearly the same as far as features go, there is always a way to differentiate. If your products are comparable in features, point out differences in after-purchase service, delivery, stability of the company backing up the product, product durability, how products are made, and reputation.

When trying to prove the uniqueness of your product against your competitors, you must be careful. You spend all your working time selling the products you represent. To you, there may be cataclysmic differences between your products and those of your competitors. But to your client, those differences may not seem so large. If you are going to get specific as to how the materials in your product are superior to those of a competitor, make sure there is a client benefit. Otherwise your client may say, "So what if you use a stronger grade of steel? Both products will do the job, and their price is lower."

Also consider that the more similar in features and price the product you sell is to your competitors', the more likely the purchase decision will be made on an emotional level, rather than on logic. If you are going to claim that your product is unique, you must be prepared to prove it. Make comparative presentations showing side-by-side features or benefits.

7. *Never negotiate a major contract with a Price Grinder over the phone.*

Telephone negotiations favor the buyer's side for several reasons:

- It's easier for your customer to say no on the phone than to your face, especially if you have traveled many miles through driving rain and are sitting in his office.
- You can't read body language or facial expressions to really know how far to concede or counter demand.
- It is less personal, which will favor the buyer.
- Telephone negotiations are faster and more to the point, with a tendency toward win-lose conclusions: "That's my best offer, take it or leave it. Call me back tomorrow with your decision . . . Click." However, if you are sitting in the client's office when you hear this, you can say, "Hey, come on, let's talk this over!"

8. *If you are being pushed into a corner, stall.*

I once started to negotiate a space contract with a client who was an extremely experienced Price Grinder. She was remarkable at ripping through all my arguments in an effort to get price concessions. Clearly, hardball negotiating was what she did all day long, ten hours a day. I spent my days merely selling. Under circumstances like this I recommend a dignified retreat. Claim that you have no authority to grant concessions like these—even if you do. Go back to your office and talk to your sales manager about the next step.

9. *Do not give in to every price demand.*

Do I even have to say this? It may seem like a no-brainer, but it does run contrary to the best instincts of many great salespeople I have worked with. When you extend good customer service to a client, you do everything possible to ensure your client's satisfaction. Any reasonable request your client makes, you see that he gets and gets quickly.

When you negotiate on price with a Price Grinder, you are entering into a part of a client relationship that is fundamentally different. For the Price Grinder, rate negotiation is a sport. Sometimes making a few extra demands on you is his way of trying to get a little extra while testing the strength of you, your product, and your company.

There is a real value trap you can fall into by keeping your "everything the client wants, the client gets" service mentality during a price negotiation. If you go plead with your boss and get the client everything he demands, you may win the battle but ultimately lose the war. While your client may be personally satisfied that he came away from the negotiation the winner, this satisfaction does not always translate into a long-term win for you.

If you are quick to make price concessions, your client's perception of the value of your product may go down. Also, if you cave in quickly just to get the business, consider what effect this will have on your client's attitude the next time he buys from you. Will he expect an even lower price?

Giving in to every demand a client makes is often viewed as weakness, not conciliation. Also, never cave in to a price concession right away. The Price Grinder will use the last price you gave him as the starting point for the next round of price negotiations. If you caved in easily last time, the pressure will be greater the next time.

10. Make a deal personally difficult to get.

Remember, it is not your client's money we are dealing with. It belongs to the company he works for. In many organizations the red tape your client would have to go through to accomplish certain tasks makes some requests doable but personally difficult. If getting a price concession involves extra difficulty for that individual, he will often stop demanding one. When I managed a sales staff, I routinely told my salespeople that we would extend a 5 percent discount to any client who would pay us for the whole year up front. Most buyers, realizing the red tape and hassle they would personally have to contend with in their organization to get a check up front, dropped their demands.

If a price concession really means enough that they will jump through this hoop, then they deserve to get it. In most cases what you are really doing is saying no while giving the appearance of continued cooperation.

11. Use him to find out what your competition is doing.

The Price Grinder will stick the details of your competition in your face. Encourage him to give you more. Take notes; this is great competitive information. But, as mentioned earlier, take price information with a grain of salt.

12. Ask about how his company views deals with its own customers who price grind on them.

Ask your client how much his company's salespeople go off their price sheets when selling their company's product. Ask what would happen to his company's profit margin and product quality if they kept price cutting for a prolonged period. Some buyers think this is a salesperson's argument and that it holds no weight in the real world. After all, everyone loves a bargain. But I have seen this argument work for some.

13. Take a step back for a reality check.

In spite of how much a Price Grinder may yell and scream about price, he will not buy because of price alone. Clients don't buy products on price; they buy products on value. In a typical business-to-business tough competitive bid, the prices offered between vendors are close. Most of the time the client has the money to buy your product. Often more time is spent discussing the least important item of all, the price.

Closing Strategies

Closing the Price Grinder is a game of poker. If you need to make a price concession, you have to know just how far to go. Eventually you really do have to say no.

1. If you make a price concession, close on it.

Before you give the Price Grinder a concession, say, "If I can get this price, will you buy?" If he says no, it's likely he won't buy at any price. If he says yes, go to your manager, get the price, and ask for the order. If you grant only a small price concession, explain that you can't go any lower than that because you have much larger clients who would take offense if they ever found out.

2. Make a nonprice concession and close on it.

Ask questions to generate other concession options. Often what is most important to your client doesn't involve price. Ultimately your client will say, "I can live with that" and accept your offer.

3. Close with no concessions.

If you are going to "just say no" to the Price Grinder without giving any concessions, you need to feel very confident of your competitive position. You should know what other vendors can offer your client and understand why it is unlikely that he will give them his business.

You may also just say no if you know your client to be a "sport" price negotiator. You can deflect his price demand with a joke and move on: "My prices are too high? But how do you expect me to buy you all those fancy lunches?"

If you are granting no concessions anywhere to anyone, explain that it is the fairest way possible. All your clients know exactly what everyone else is paying and getting. This approach has special appeal for small accounts. More flexible price negotiations will favor the bigger accounts who have more leverage.

2

The Client Who
Will Not See You

From the Tough Calls survey:

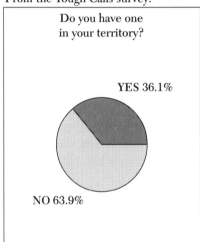

Do you have one
in your territory?

YES 36.1%

NO 63.9%

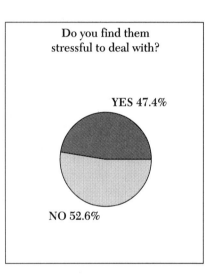

Do you find them
stressful to deal with?

YES 47.4%

NO 52.6%

"It cancels the opportunity to help a company."

Business Writer, Albany, N.Y.

When your first phone call is not returned you don't think much about it, but after several instances of having your phone calls not taken or returned, you realize that this person is not going to see you. There are a lot of reasons why clients avoid meeting with salespeople. It's reasonable to assume that whomever you are calling on is called upon by a lot of different salespeople, and that if this person spent all her time meeting with just the people who call on her, she wouldn't be able to get the rest of her job done. But, here's the thing: She is probably meeting with some salespeople, and you just are not one of them. Before you can give your presentation, before you can overcome objections, before you can even attempt any kind of close, you have to get in.

Pitfalls

1. Taking it personally.

It's not a personal thing when a client refuses to see you. It could be that the timing is off. It could be that your approach is off. It could be a lot of different things. Don't take it personally—take it as a signal that it's time to stop and rethink before you try again.

2. Becoming so persistent that you become a nuisance.

Again, there is a reason why this person has not met with you the first time you called. Just because you call a dozen more times does not mean that the underlying dynamic that is preventing you from getting in has changed. Sometimes trying a different tack can be a good approach. It's hard to know how to be persistent without being offensive. Any salesperson worth her salt is going to overstep those bounds once in a while. I have had several experiences where clients have flat-out told me that I'm just calling them too often. As a salesperson you are given a little more latitude in these kinds of situations than if you were just, say, a casual friend. As one client told me, "I want to know that you want my business." Sometimes being persistent, even to a fault, is OK, but if a client tells you flat-out that you are calling too much, it's time to back off.

3. Giving up after the first few attempts.

An unprecedented sale usually takes a few visits to make. An unprecedented sales call usually takes a few attempts to secure. If it were easy, there would be no need for salespeople. The orders would just show up in the mail!

4. Passing judgment on a client who has passed judgment on you.

I've seen salespeople fall into this defensive psychological state: "That woman won't see me! Boy, is she a creep. She doesn't know what she is doing, and she doesn't know what I can do for her." Really, this isn't productive thinking. Clients are busy, have lots of people calling on them, and are probably under a lot of pressure. As the salesperson, your job is to sell. It's the client's job to buy. Like it or not, and unfair or not, she has the right to pass judgment on you, not the other way around.

Selling Strategies

1. Ask yourself, "If I were in her shoes, why would I see me?"

Again, remember, she could probably get rate sheets and information about your product through the mail. In fact, she may already have them. There has to be something more to the equation than just the basics, because this time the basics aren't working. Whatever you have done to get to this point, stop and think it through again. Whatever appeal you have used is not working. You need a different appeal. Imagine that you are in this person's situation. Why would she want to see you? If you say, "Well, she wants to see me because she wants to buy what I am selling," think again. If she's not letting you in, either she is satisfied with the service of a competitor, or she has never considered how your product can be helpful. Before she will see you, you have to plan what you are going to bring to the table that offers some advantage that she is not already getting.

2. Send a letter.

If you can determine just what you can offer this client, put it in a letter and mail it to her. Letters have a lot of advantages over the telephone when it comes to getting appointments. If your client is busy, she can read and respond to the letter according to her time frame, unlike a telephone call that demands immediate attention. Also, a letter can state your case concisely and briefly and get the whole thing thought out before being interrupted in midstream because the client is in a meeting. Explain why you want to meet with her, suggest several times that would be convenient for you, and ask for the appointment.

3. *Don't leave messages.*

If you are having trouble getting through to a client, leaving messages is a real no-no. First of all, for whatever reason, this client is avoiding your calls. Leaving a trail of messages is not going to help you in any real way. The client already knows that you are trying to reach her and has your phone number. When you call the next few times to see whether you can make contact, don't leave a message; just tell the secretary that you will call back. You have to take responsibility for making the contact. Don't assume that a client who has already demonstrated that she is too busy, or too indifferent, to take your call is going to return a call. So leave a few messages, but don't leave many more.

4. *Send a nonsales-related item to the client and call to see whether she got it.*

If you can find an interesting article about this person's company, her hobby, her surname, her profession, her products, cut it out and mail it to her. This will do several things. First of all, it will set you apart from the other peddlers clamoring for her time. Secondly, it will attempt to make some kind of connection on a more significant level than, "I'm here to sell you something. Why won't you see me?" It also gives you an excuse to contact this client to see whether she received the article you mailed her.

5. *Call early in the morning and after five o'clock.*

It's been my experience that people who have a lot of authority usually don't work nine to five. Typically, they start work much earlier and are usually in their office until about six o'clock. I have always found that eight-thirty in the morning and five-thirty at night are the two best times to get important people on the phone. Usually, their secretaries are gone and a lot of the support staff that runs interference is not around. Plus, you set yourself apart as being more of a peer. If this person works until six o'clock every night, she may relate to you better if she can get hold of you in that time frame.

6. Worship her secretary.

If you are having trouble getting in to see this person, there is someone who you can befriend who can help: the woman's secretary. Secretaries are an unappreciated lot. Most are not treated with a lot of respect or paid well. Yet I have visited many companies where it is the executive secretaries who seem to be really running things. The more disorganized the client you are calling on, the more important the secretary, in terms of getting in. Many secretaries actually set the appointment schedules for their bosses. Even if they do not, they certainly know when the boss will be in town and can tell you what the best times are to give a call. If you remember a secretary's name, extend the courtesy of just getting to know her a bit when you are calling. If you do get that appointment, take some time to introduce yourself to the secretary when you come in. If she helps you get the call, send a thank-you note for helping you get it. Always remember her name. Ask about such details as favorite photographs on her desk when you visit.

7. Make a nonsales contact to help formulate your getting-in strategy.

If you are at a trade show or have occasion to meet anyone else from this organization besides the person that you are calling on, you might casually talk about what you are trying to sell the company. That other person may be able to help you understand any buying reluctance that company has to your product and your company. It may help you formulate a better getting-in strategy.

8. Subtly appeal to higher, unbiased motives.

In a perfect world every client would have a perfect understanding of every product she can buy that will do her company some good. In a perfect world every client would have a personal relationship with every salesperson who calls on her. In a perfect world every client would have enough time to meet with every salesperson who wants to make a call on her. Needless to say, we don't live in a perfect world. However, it is to the advantage of every client to know what her options are and the new developments of the products she buys. It's always worth including some sort of statement when you are trying to get in, like, "It's important for you to keep up to date with the kinds of developments of the products I'm selling. It's important for you to know what kinds of opportunities we are offering you." In a perfect world these are all good things.

9. Make a scene.

I do not recommend this and avoid it myself. However, I have known salespeople who can pull this sort of thing off. If they don't get an appointment, somehow they make a scene. They send letters to other people in the company, complaining that they can't get in. Personally, I think this is a terrible way to do things. I honestly don't know why it works, and yet I know several salespeople who use this routinely and make it succeed. I think the ability to pull this off really has to do with the personality of the salesperson. These people have a keen ability to pick up on the insecurity of a buyer and exploit it by using the implied threat of a confrontation. If you are dealing with an insecure buyer, this might work. However, I recommend against it.

10. Join a trade association.

No matter what product you are involved with, there has to be a trade association of some kind that deals with the products you are involved with. Join that association. Volunteer for a committee, or if the people you are calling on live in a specific geographic region, find out where they socialize. If you go to trade shows, ask a friendly secretary which hotel your client is staying in and see that you stay in that hotel. Joining trade associations is extra work, but if you can rub elbows with some of the people you are calling on in a nonsales environment, it always translates into a better chance of getting in.

11. Stop acting like a salesperson.

Sometimes clients avoid salespeople just because they hate all of the closing games and shenanigans we all use. Often they avoid calls because they don't want to be pressured. The other issue is that very often a lot of the salespeople who have called on them in the past have simply wasted their time. Somehow you have to make it clear that you are a cut above those salespeople and that sitting down with you is going to be productive. Here is where it really pays to know more about your product, the industry, and the product's uses than can be described in the company literature. If you can position yourself as being more of a buyer's consultant than a salesperson, you will have a much easier time getting in. If you can position yourself as someone who can help a client through the buying process and make her look like a hero, you will motivate her to see you.

12. Use a creative getting-in technique.

In industries where I've sold, there used to be a lot more of this than there is today. I think there is more pressure on people who buy products today and more pressure on salespeople as well. In the industries I've sold ten and fifteen years ago, there used to be a lot more long lunches and schmoozing and a lot less meat-and-potatoes dialogue. However, I'm still a big fan of creative getting-in techniques, but their use seems to be a lot less common today.

I was once having trouble getting in to visit a buyer and wrote her a clever poem that I sent along with flowers. Even though I had been trying to get her on the phone for an entire month, she returned my call the minute she got the flowers. Creative getting-in techniques are a way to help you stand out from the crowd. I believe the key to using them is to do something that is specifically appropriate for the situation and not just creative for creativity's sake.

I was once having trouble getting the attention of a buyer when I noticed that at his booth at a trade show all of his salespeople wore tuxedos. When I talked with one of the representatives of this company, it seemed that this had been a tradition at this company for many years. These salespeople's attitude was,

"We take our customers so seriously that we dress this way to honor them as they visit our trade show booth." The next time I called on this company I wore a tuxedo. Even though I had never been able to make a call successfully before, I had a terrific call the day I wore my tuxedo. But if this had just been any old company and I had showed up in a tuxedo just for a lark, I honestly don't know whether it would have had the same effect another time.

I have also heard some getting-in stories that ended in disaster. One salesperson, who had been frozen out of a major account after a blunder, decided he would try to make peace with the client. What he did was mail them a dove in a box. This may have seemed like a creative idea, but what happened was that the dove, who had been scrunched up in this box all day long, got quite hysterical when the client opened it. The dove flew at the client and pecked him in the head. The salesperson's peace offering ended in disaster.

If you can think of a creative getting-in technique that has unique appeal to that company, or that person, it's always a great way to try again. Just don't send any claustrophobic doves!

13. Sit down and ask yourself some questions.

Ask, "Is this the right person to call on?" It is altogether possible that the reason you're not getting in is because she is not the person who buys your product at this company. This is the sort of thing that a friendly secretary, office peer, or coworker can tip you off to.

Ask, "Is this the right time to be calling?" If you sell a product that is considered capital goods that will have to be written into next year's budget, there may be a specific time that the client will want to hear from you, and that time may not be now. You might just ask what time frame might be more appropriate for your next contact.

Ask, "Am I selling what she wants to buy?" This is actually a much more complicated question than it might seem at first. If you were selling a cleaning service you might say, "It's obvious, she might need a cleaning service, the company has a building," but the truth is, that client can buy a cleaning service from a lot of different sources. What she really might want to buy is a way to make herself look better in front of her boss, or a way to lower costs, or a way to find a friend to talk to, or a way to feel more important in an area where she has some power, or a way to position herself with her company as a smart buyer who can move up the corporate ladder. We're talking about getting beyond the physical product or service that you're selling and tapping in to the emotional needs that might be satisfied by buying from you.

It is difficult to do this before you have even met this person, but sometimes it's possible to discover these kinds of things by talking to other colleagues of yours who have called on this account, by checking old call reports from people who have called on this account before you, or by talking to other personnel at the company who work with this person. Sometimes getting friendly with the client's secretary can be all-revealing. If you listen carefully to a secretary when she talks about her boss, you can discover many things about that person's emotional state. I have gleaned a lot of important tips from secretaries in their lighthearted, offhand comments. One secretary told me, in a joking sort of way, "I think he is in a bad mood today, look out." Over the course of a few weeks, when I tried to contact this man, it was clear that she was reporting on a client who had emotional ups and downs and periodically needed to assert authority in an almost bombastic fashion. Although I had never spoken to this client, I was being painted an emotional picture of just who he was.

Another administrative assistant I called on was clearly in awe of her boss. In our brief conversations about him she would pepper our conversation with comments about just how inspired and amazed she was at this man's abilities. At one point she told me, "I think he's a truly great man; he's a teacher, he's a friend, he's a visionary." The fact that I couldn't get him on the phone or get an appointment with him was one thing, but an emotional picture of this man was being painted for me. A man like this might like to meet with me if I presented a case for fair play or offered to share some big ideas about the industry his product serves. For the bombastic boss you might pepper your getting-in letter with a sense of humility and wanting to serve the person you're calling on.

Psyching out the emotional state of the person you are trying to get in to see can often be an effective strategy. The question is, when you approach a client for an appointment, are you selling emotionally what the client wants to buy? There are a lot of ways you can get to know a client emotionally without ever meeting her. If you're sensitive to the organization you are interacting with, you can gain an understanding about how she operates, even before meeting her or speaking with her.

14. Stop calling for a while.

If you can't get anywhere, just put the client on the back burner for two months. Most salespeople have a tickler file for situations where they just can't get through. Call these clients again in two months and your luck may change.

15. Say, "I'll be in the building. Can I come see you?"

A lot of clients don't like the pressure on them of believing that you made a special trip just to see them. If you make it clear that you are going to be traveling in their area, in their neighborhood, in their city, on a specific date and that stopping by would be little effort for you, sometimes they will see you. Send a fax, leave a message, but be specific that you will be in the area at a specific time and date, and ask whether it would be convenient to pay a visit. The worst that can happen is that they will say no.

16. Drop off something personal at her office.

A great way to get to know the woman's secretary, or the person who works most closely with her in the office environment, is to pay a visit to that office. Of course, if you don't have an appointment, this is difficult to do; but what if you're just stopping by to drop off something? If it's around Christmas, tell her secretary that you'll be stopping by to drop off a corporate present. Go buy a bottle of wine or a fruitcake on your expense account and drop it by. While you are there you will build rapport with the secretary, if only for a brief time, and also psych out the environment.

17. Research the company.

There are a tremendous number of resources available to anyone who wants to sit down and look them up. Go to your local library and look up the company you are calling on in *Standard and Poor's* or *Hoovers Business Resources,* or do a search on the Internet. It's not difficult these days to come up with some kind of information about the company you are calling on. Sometimes you can discover something about the company that might give you an edge or a rationale for a visit, or you might just get the attention of the person you are calling on by providing her with some piece of information about her company that she didn't know.

Closing Strategies

1. Be specific.

Closing the client who will not see you means asking for an appointment and getting it. The best way to get an appointment is to be as specific as possible. If you have the client on the phone, propose a specific time. "I'll be in your area next week— on Thursday. Can I see you at 10:00 A.M.?" If you are acting through an intermediary, such as a secretary, it's often helpful to provide two options. "Can I meet with her next week, Thursday at 10:00 A.M., or the week after that, Monday at 11:00 A.M.?" Your job is to provide a specific time that the client can react to. This focuses her attention on a time to meet as opposed to whether she should meet with you at all.

2. Promise a benefit.

As you approach getting an appointment, say, "I will show you a way to save money," or "I will show you a way to increase the efficiency of your operation." Whatever it is your product will do for this person, make a commitment that you will demonstrate a benefit.

3. Make a time commitment.

When you ask for an appointment, tell the client that you will not waste her time or that you will take no more than fifteen minutes. When you get to the appointment, take off your watch, put it on the table and tell her that you will take no longer than ten minutes of her time. Usually, when you get to the person's office, she will willingly spend more time with you than you asked for, if you have a compelling story.

4. Think about the next time.

Once you finally get in, the thing that you absolutely must do before you leave that office is come up with a hook to get back in another time. It's not just enough to get into the person's office once. You have to come up with a reason for another visit: a specific quote, information that she wants about your product, something personal about a hobby that you both share. As you leave, make sure that you can get back in another time.

3

The Client Who
Lies to You

From the Tough Calls survey:

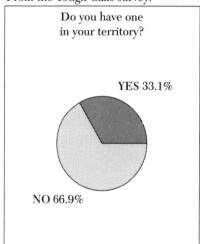

Do you have one
in your territory?

YES 33.1%

NO 66.9%

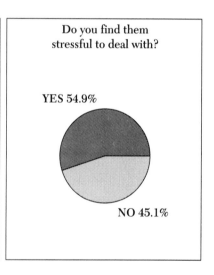

Do you find them
stressful to deal with?

YES 54.9%

NO 45.1%

"I cannot objectively address what is preventing the sale."
Company President, power switching equipment, Boston, Mass.

I called the client to see whether I could get one last order in October. He told me it was too late, the budget for my project was shot, and there would be no more orders placed for the rest of the year. I offered a delayed billing plan so that he could place his order now and not get billed until January of the following year, when his new budget would be in place. "A billing extension will not make a difference," he said. "I am placing no more orders until next year." I made a note to call him later and moved on. One Friday in December at 5:15 P.M., a friend of mine who worked at that company ruined my weekend by tipping me off that a direct competitor had gotten an order by offering his company a delayed billing plan like the one I had been told would not make a difference. I was furious. "He lied to me!" I raged and ranted to anyone who would listen to me all weekend long. When Monday came and I called the client, he explained to me that my competitor was smart enough to write that delayed billing program into his contract six months earlier. At the time he turned me down, it had already been in place for three months. Maybe it was subtle, but at the time I spoke with him he could have told me that he had already accepted a delayed billing program with a competitor of mine and would not accept a *second* delayed billing program.

As you approach a situation where it looks as if your client has lied to you, don't confront. Instead pursue a dialogue. Look for answers to the easy questions, such as, Did things change between now and your last conversation? Did you really understand what he told you? If it was just a misunderstanding and you have cleared it up, great. Here are four situations that account for most of the "lying" by clients that I have encountered.

1. *Things have changed and you are out of the decision-making loop.* On Monday the buyer tells you, "Don't worry, your order will come through next week." On Tuesday the budget gets slashed and your proposal is no longer being considered. You coast merrily through the week expecting an order the following week. Did the client lie? The better question is, when did you find out about the budget cut? Did you find out when you called for the order and heard that you weren't getting it? Or did the client call and tip you off that a budget cut was in the works with enough time for you to defend your proposal constructively?

2. *You are dealing with a client who is out of the loop.* If a client tells you a lot of things that just don't pan out, it is possible that that person is just not in the decision-making process. If he doesn't seem to have the right information, it is probable that he is not seriously involved. Typically you are dealing with someone insecure in his position who wants to appear more involved than he is.

3. *It's easy to misunderstand things in a sound-bite relationship.* As clients come under more and more pressure to get things done, my conversations with them seem to last less and less time. I have many working relationships with clients whom I talk to frequently, but with each conversation lasting only a few minutes. It's easy to misunderstand things under these circumstances.

4. *You are dealing with a client who is hopelessly disorganized.* Sometimes the reason a client tells you one thing and then something different happens is that he forgot to follow through. Disorganized clients are very dangerous; if they goof up you are the one who suffers.

But if you have a long memory or just keep good notes, you will find that a few of your clients regularly "lie" to you. They will routinely tell you that one thing is going to happen and then something quite different does. They take liberties in the buyer-seller relationship and hold back key pieces of information that would help you sell by letting you know where you stand.

Pitfalls

1. Calling your client a liar.

You just cannot do this, although you might fantasize about doing it. If you did, it might feel good for the moment, but it could destroy your relationship with someone whom you will still have to call on next week. After all is said and done, he is still the client and you are still the person who calls on him. If your client is giving you incomplete or misleading information, it is not his problem, it is yours.

2. Putting the client on the defensive.

How do you react when it looks as if your client has lied to you? If it was just a misunderstanding and you come on strong, you can look like a jerk. If you make a big stink, you will probably encourage the very kind of behavior you want to eliminate. Your client might think, "Boy, I did this salesperson a favor by sharing this information, then he gets it mixed up and makes a big scene. Who needs it!" If you alienate your client, you have just lost a customer who will still be buying from someone else.

Selling Strategies

1. Ask yourself, "How can I become more important to this client?"

If your client is consistently giving you incomplete or misleading information, he could be sending you a message about your relationship with him. Your client may think that the extra time it takes to give you honest feedback and extra disclosure is effort with no benefit. If you bring nothing of value to the table for him and you are viewed as a potential problem if things do not go your way, he may naturally want to limit the time he spends with you. A little white lie here and there is often the time-saving shortcut he will use to get you out of his hair. He might say, "We are not buying your product right now—I don't even have budgets," but he may know that he will have his budget handed to him tomorrow. How you can become a more valuable person for the client depends on you and the client. I recommend taking a step back and seeing whether there are ways to make some service calls where you pursue a helping dialogue and not actually try to sell him anything.

2. Forgive him.

This is a reality check. You are one of many people trying to sell products to this client. Even if your client does not share enough information with you about what is going on, there may be other salespeople whom he does keep in the loop. I find that in order to keep working toward the goal of becoming one of these more-in-the-loop players, I need to consciously forgive him and adjust my attitude. It does not matter who made the mistake. If there is a follow-up sale, I will still be the salesperson and he will still be the client, and if I am carrying a grudge it will not help me sell this client.

3. Clear the air.

Depending on your relationship with your client, you might try one of these three levels of approaches toward clearing the air.

Level 1: Ask for clarification. When you think you have been lied to, this is the place to start. Ask for clarification, explain that there was a miscommunication and you want to clear it up. Tell him what you thought he said, ask him to explain what actually happened, then shut up and let him do the talking.

Level 2: Explain your embarrassment. If you have a relationship with your customer, why not use it? If you want to "lean" a little more into your client, you can call on the salesperson's best leaning tool, guilt. As above, explain to your client that what he said would happen did not happen. Tell your client that you shared his initial conversation with your boss or coworkers, and when his commitment or order did not come through, it was a big disappointment and even a professional embarrassment as well. Without placing blame on the client for holding back information, just explain that this situation, however it happened, caused you some embarrassment. Finish up by saying, "I hope this never happens again."

Level 3: Question your relationship. I have never done this, but have seen other salespeople work it masterfully. Here you take guilt to the next level. Usually I see this used only with clients with whom the salesperson has an extremely good relationship. Say in hurt or angry tones, "Mark, when your order did not come through I was shocked. I know that things change, but I would have expected that after all these years the least you would have done was to give me a call," and so on.

If the above do not work for you and you find that you are dealing with a client who really does misrepresent things, try these.

4. Cover yourself with paper.

There is something about committing details of conversations to paper that keeps dishonest clients honest. Somehow a paper trail sets up a psychological barrier that many deceitful clients will not cross. Paper is the best defense against clients who withhold or misrepresent information. If they agree to review a sales proposal by next Friday, send them a letter or fax them a note thanking them for their cooperation and mention the Friday "deadline." Sending a thank-you note is always a nice thing to do, but in the case of a client who regularly misrepresents things it is more than a nicety. Here the thank-you note informally documents the agreement. If there is a dispute over what was agreed to later on, you might say, "But Jim, you agreed to review the proposal by Friday. Remember, I was so excited about the fact that I sent you a thank-you note." Needless to say, any actual orders you get from a client who misrepresents things should also be documented on paper.

5. Start a journal.

You remember the client told you that you would get the order in March and that it was a done deal. Months later in March when you do not get the order, the client says that what he really meant was that in March it was a done deal that he would again resubmit your proposal. You may have dozens of clients and you might be handling hundreds of transactions a month. Do you remember exactly what each one said to you? I find it hard to remember exact details months later, unless I write them down. For your own sanity, this is advisable. I use sales contact software so it is easy to take a few extra notes. If you are not computerized, start a journal of your clients who regularly misrepresent things, and take extensive notes. I got one misrepresenting client back on track by saying something like, "But Frank, I have in my notes that on October 23, 1995, you mentioned that you were expecting a larger increase than normal, and that this would result in your needing to place an order right around now." By citing specific dates, numbers, and comments that the client made, very often you can jog his memory.

Closing Strategies

The "sale" you are trying to make with the client who lies to you is that you will not be lied to again.

1. Make sure the same thing won't happen next time.

A "misunderstanding" occurred. Your client either withheld or misrepresented information that put you at a disadvantage in the selling process. You have a dialogue, you clear things up. The real question is, will the same thing happen again when you pursue follow-up sales? Part of your dialogue as you finish up clearing the air should be about next time, and how the two of you can take steps to prevent this from happening again.

2. Ask for the commitment of a warning phone call.

As I mentioned earlier, the real question is not whether things will change, because they always will. The real question is when your client will tell you about them. Did he tell you after the fact when it was too late to do anything, or in the actual process so that you could react constructively? Tell your client that you understand that it is unrealistic to expect him to call you every five minutes every time your proposal gets into difficulty through the process of buying, but if it looks as if things are really starting to unravel for your proposal, ask your client for the courtesy of a phone call. Sometimes he will give it to you.

3. Ask for a relationship among equals.

Many clients take advantage of the buyer-seller relationship and really do not give it much thought. But if you have a client on whom you are spending a lot of extra time to service him exceptionally well, ask him to do a little work on his end to help you continue that servicing. Tell him you need regular feedback on the buying process. Sometimes explaining that you would like a relationship based on mutual self-interest makes this kind of impression.

4

The Client Who
Has No Buying
Authority

From the Tough Calls survey:

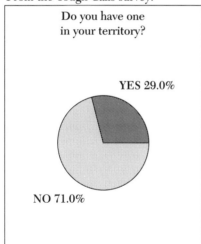

**Do you have one
in your territory?**

YES 29.0%

NO 71.0%

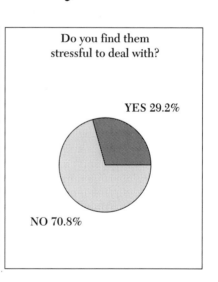

**Do you find them
stressful to deal with?**

YES 29.2%

NO 70.8%

*"I get buying signals from the person I call on, but everything
has to be okayed by management. My product is complex and
management doesn't understand the costs involved."*

Truck Leasing Salesman, Des Moines, Iowa

*"You feel like you have built a relationship on false pretenses
when the client cannot pull the (buying) trigger like he leads you
to believe he can."*

Advertising Salesman, Chicago, Ill.

In sales, things are often not what they seem. I remember starting on one sales territory and meeting with a lot of professional clients who seemed to be in command of their destinies. After I had worked the territory for about two years, though, I realized that about three-quarters of the people assigned to meet with me had no direct buying authority whatsoever. Most were information gatherers who would channel data to the people who did the buying. The real buyers didn't have time to meet with all the salespeople who called on them. Still, I found the support of these nonbuyers to be critical to my sales efforts. Although they could not say yes to my proposals, they were inside the companies I was trying to sell, and I was not. Their perspective and advice often made the difference between shaping a sales proposal that lived or one that died. And I always knew that even if they couldn't say yes to my proposals, they could torpedo my efforts with the people who could say yes, because they had direct access to them and I did not.

Pitfalls

1. Assuming that because the client is assigned to meet with you, she has buying authority.

The answer to the direct question, "Are you a decision maker?" is always, "Yes." Many clients who have no buying authority do not like to admit it. An insecure client may be afraid that admitting this will weaken her hand if she needs to ask you for a favor or a concession. Next week her boss may call her in and tell her to cancel an order or to get a time extension from you. How quickly will you return her calls or grant a concession if you know she has no buying authority? She may think it is to her advantage to keep her mouth shut and let you believe she is more involved than she is. Very often, the more a client proclaims her influence and boasts about her expertise, the more she is bluffing. Sometimes it's the buyers who ask questions quietly who have the real buying authority.

2. Thinking of her as an insignificant obstacle, not as an important gatekeeper.

I know many salespeople who view clients with no buying authority with disdain and immediately try to go around them. If the real decision maker does not meet with you directly, she has a reason. Often, if she spent time meeting with you and every other salesperson, she would never get any work done. Out of necessity, she puts a gatekeeper in place to field the routine pitches and find the few sales proposals or ideas worthy of more dialogue. From the real decision maker's point of view, a salesperson who immediately goes around the gatekeeper will probably be viewed as a nuisance.

When I start to get frustrated with a client with no buying authority, I find that if I think of her as a gatekeeper and not as an obstacle, I can adjust my attitude and behavior appropriately.

3. Going over her head without considering the consequences.

Few things in sales are more difficult than knowing when to go over someone's head. I always like to look at the long-term consequences. Before you consider doing it, ask yourself the following questions:

- *Do I really have something to say to this person's boss that will make a difference?* Put your ego aside and seriously consider this question.
- *Will the person whom I've gone over be offended?* Strange things happen in sales. Unimportant people who stay with companies get promoted to positions of higher authority. Bosses leave and people are promoted into their slots. Maybe this person can't help you to make a sale today, but what about tomorrow?
- *What is the worst-case scenario, and what are the potential benefits?* The salesperson who says, "I don't have anything to lose because I am not getting any business" is often creating a self-fulfilling prophecy.

Selling Strategies

1. Motivate her to admit that she is not the decision maker.

Some clients will immediately volunteer this information in the first five minutes of the call. With others, you will have to smoke it out over time. But once this admission gets made, your relationship fundamentally changes for the better. Immediately, the goal shifts from you selling the person in the room directly, to you selling the real decision maker with the help of that person.

2. Smoke her out.

Here are several approaches to finding gatekeepers who are not admitting their status:

  a. *Ask for the order.* Only a real decision maker can give you any kind of commitment. If she can't, ask her who else you need to speak with to get one. The name she gives you is that of the decision maker you may have to persuade.
  b. *Ask for details about how buying decisions were made last year.* Admitting that she doesn't know what went on last year may seem innocent enough, but consider that if she wasn't involved in last year's decisions, she may not be involved in this year's.
  c. *Ask her about budgets.* Sometimes these numbers are confidential, and the client may tell you that. But if a client tells you that she is not involved with budgets, she has made a statement on how involved she is in the buying process. If she does not know what the budget is, she may not be in the decision-making loop.
  d. *Go with instinct.* I sometimes just get a feeling that the person is not really in a position to buy. The problem here is that often you give your instinct too much credit. Just because she asks dumb questions and does not seem qualified to buy does not mean she is not doing the buying.

e. *After you have given your presentation, ask whether there is anyone else who should see this information.* If there is, tell her you would be glad to mail a copy of the presentation or leave one behind, if she will give the person's name to you.

f. *Ask everyone you meet on the account about how decisions get made.* I once found out what was really going on in a company by gaining the confidence of an especially observant secretary. The person you call on may be defensive about giving you an honest answer. But her coworkers, peers, and members of the support staff may be more candid.

3. Become a sales trainer.

She wants to buy your product but does not have the authority to do so. But you are in a position to share a body of expertise that can help her. You can teach her how to sell, and more specifically how to sell your product to her company. Tell her that as a salesperson you are uniquely qualified to coach her. Ask her what her selling challenges are. Ask what she has tried already and what has worked in the past. Give her the information she needs to back up her selling efforts.

4. Arrange for a joint call.

Ask your contact to set you up a joint call with the real decision maker. Suggest to her that by doing this she will not be put in the position of having to make decisions that she is not involved in. Or suggest that she will look good by bringing these ideas to her boss's attention.

5. Come up with important information that her boss will want to see.

Your company may do studies that are of interest to your customers, or you can get book smart and find an important study or report that your client's boss will want to see.

The danger is that the information gatherer may view your report as a real plum that she can pick and pass on to her boss.

If this happens, you may have spent a lot of time to get information that wins you nothing but the fleeting gratitude of the information gatherer. No good! Instead use the report to sell the idea of a higher-level meeting. Tell her about the report, but do not take it with you on the call. Describe how you believe it will offer insight that her boss will appreciate. Also, you have to position yourself as bringing some added value to the presentation of the report. Tell her it isn't the kind of report that you can just drop in the mail, it has to be presented.

6. Come up with a big idea that demands her boss's attention.

If you sell by routine, your sales proposals will be handled by routine. If you are trying make an unprecedented sale, the routine approach can be a one-way ticket to oblivion. Coming up with the big idea is not easy, though. Many ideas that might seem pretty big to you might not seem so big to your client. Brainstorm with other people in your company to see whether there is something you can develop.

7. Prove it on paper.

Gatekeepers channel information to the decision makers. It is to your advantage to make your case as powerful as you can when it flows through the channel. Paper can travel well through those channels. If you put your story on paper, you can tell it exactly the way you want it told. But ask yourself whether the material you are sending can sell your product without you. It may have to.

8. Send copies of your letters to other buying influences.

It may be in bad taste to go over someone's head, but it is less difficult to send an extra copy of your correspondence to other people in the organization. It's a lot less threatening, and it may get your message across just as effectively.

9. Go over her head.

Do you feel that you have no choice but to go over your client's head? Going over someone's head is always risky, and you should weigh what can be gained and what can be lost. My point is not that you should never do it. Eventually, every salesperson has to go over someone's head to fight for her product and company. It's not a question of should you, it's a question of when you do, how should you do it. Here are some approaches to think about.

■ *Build trust.* One way to go over someone's head is by enlisting her cooperation. If you befriend the person you are calling on and truly understand that she does not have the authority to buy anything from you, at some point you may say, "Look, I know you don't have the authority to buy what I'm selling, but your boss does. Is it possible that you can get us an appointment together, and the three of us can then decide what to do?" If the person you call on is on your side and is not threatened by this kind of overture, she will help you to get that appointment.

■ *Have your boss make the contact.* This is the cleanest way to do things, if you have to continue working with the person you're now calling on. If your boss calls on her boss, there's a symmetry that causes less offense. In difficult situations, where you feel that you have to get around the person you're calling on, having your boss call on her boss is a good approach.

■ *Wait for vacations and sick days to make your contact.* I can't tell you how well this approach works. Casually bring up vacations on your next call and find out when your client is going on vacation. Make a point to have some small detail that needs to be handled when that person is away. Typically, her boss will be handling the calls and may get involved with that detail. When this happens, you may have some fascinating little piece of information or tidbit that you think the boss will find interesting. Use this opportunity to establish some kind of rapport—that you can then try to exploit.

■ *Move laterally before you move up.* Try finding someone else in the organization whom you can talk to about the objections you've been handed. Are the objections real? Are there ways to get around them?

■ *Try the frontal assault.* Say, "Look, I hear what you say, but I don't agree with you. I hope you won't be offended, but I feel that I have to take this matter up with someone else." This approach is direct and honest but works only when you already have a relationship with your client's boss. If you don't, it is likely that your client will block your efforts to get to the boss.

I have never used this technique, and I believe it will likely create a confrontational relationship with the person you are going to have to call on again. I have seen salespeople use it successfully, however. Most often they have both an insecure client and a relationship with the client's boss.

Closing Strategies

The person you're calling on cannot buy, but she is still is the person you have to call on. How do you get a commitment from someone who cannot make one? Consider that the organization's structure was created for a reason. It was not meant to block all sales from happening, just to keep the people who buy from wasting too much of their time meeting with people who sell.

1. Put all of your sales proposals in writing, then send them to the person you call on; include multiple copies.

Acknowledge that the contact has to go to others to get the order. Make it easy for her. Very often, she will not be able to articulate your sales position in just the way you want it to be presented. But if you put it in writing and use her as a conduit, then at least you will get a fair hearing.

2. Be very sensitive to timing.

The person you're calling on is dependent on other people to make the decision. These people have travel schedules and other work to do. She must approach them at strategic times to get the decision. Always ask such questions as, "When will the decision be made? Whom else will you be meeting with? Do you know when you will be meeting with these people? At what time do you think you will have some kind of feedback as to how the decision is going?" The truly scary thing about dealing with a gatekeeper is that you have very little control over how the decision-making process unfolds. You may give the person you call on a terrific presentation. She may go into a meeting three weeks later with three vice-presidents who may ask her questions that she does not know how to respond to concerning your proposal. Two days later, there may be a final meeting where all proposals are considered and the winners are sorted out. If you can get to your contact during that two-day break, you have the opportunity to get new information to her that may save the day. But if you are locked out of the decision-making time line, then you will have completely lost control of the buying process.

Ultimately, the organization will buy products through this indirect method. Your job is to figure out how best to influence the process.

5

The Client Who
Loves What You Say,
Then Does Not Buy

From the Tough Calls survey:

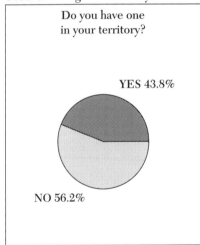

Do you have one
in your territory?

YES 43.8%

NO 56.2%

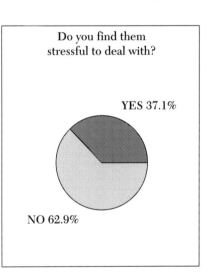

Do you find them
stressful to deal with?

YES 37.1%

NO 62.9%

"The deception is frustrating. They give the appearance of being ready to buy, then back away for whatever reason."

Salesman, investment services and materials,
Scranton-Wilkes Barre, Pa.

In a profession full of daily rejection, visiting her was like taking a vacation. She asked whether she could get you coffee. She thanked you for your presentation. She made you feel that you were doing such a good job. Everything was going so well, then—whammo!—she went and bought from someone else. You should have seen it coming, but you didn't. She may be uncomfortable telling you "no" to your face, or she may have no problem with confrontation at all but does not want to deal with the time-consuming process of explaining her objections to you and having you respond. For her, it is easier to offer no resistance on the call, then quietly go off and buy somewhere else. Your job is to spot her early and deepen the selling dialogue, even if it means making her a little uncomfortable at first. Experienced salespeople develop a radar sense that spots this client coming. You can too.

Pitfalls

1. Mistaking her for a relationship sell.

The closer in price and features the product you sell is to those of your competitors, the more likely your client will buy for emotional rather than logical reasons. The essence of this relationship sell is that the client buys from the salesperson and company that the client has the best feeling about. Here is a client who is willing to be your friend immediately. If you assume this to be a relationship sell, you might figure that you have the sale in the bag. Nothing could be further from the truth. With this client it's really easy to make a friend without making a sale.

2. Assuming that she has been sold because there have been no objections.

With most clients the last thing you want to do is bring up objections yourself. Why bring up trouble and introduce a problem that may not have existed before? But any serious buyer is going to have some objections as she fits her needs into your products. Raising objections is a natural part of the process of buying. If none are raised that's a warning sign that something is wrong.

3. *Mistaking the nice things she says for buying signals.*

With a normal client, positive comments really are buying signals that tell you that you are heading for a sale. With this client, they simply aren't. There is something else going on here. She may have a lousy personal life, where no one cares about her. You walk in the door and soak up every word she says, and have positive things to say about many things. She may be insecure in her job and looking for reinforcement anywhere she can get it. She may be fronting for the real decision maker who does not want to be identified and will be upset with her if he is. She may have no intention of ever buying from you and is being extra nice to you because she likes you and wants to let you down easy. Whatever it is, if you play the game her way, and react the way salespeople are traditionally trained to react, you will lose big. Your job is to spot her early and react appropriately. To recap:

    a. The client raised no objections on the call.
    b. Your call seemed too short to really convince someone to buy, even though she said she would.
    c. You made a real personal connection on your call but you did not talk much about business.
    d. She just seemed a little too "nice," almost as if she were apologizing for something.
    e. She didn't raise the typical objections that a client like her typically raises. In short, it seemed just a little too easy.

Selling Strategies

1. *Deepen the selling dialogue from a friendly visit to a business call.*

Accept the friendly facade, but somehow you have to get to the real buying issues. You don't have to offend, but you do have to initiate a deeper, more businesslike dialogue. I have found, in most cases, that she will respond to this positively. The truth is that even though she is resisting a more businesslike call, on some level she does expect you to pursue one and is probably well prepared to deal with one once it is initiated. Making the transition from this friendly visit to the more businesslike call can be handled in several ways. For a soft transition, ask a general question about the buying process, then let the response guide your transition into a more serious dialogue: "Mary, I have a question for you. Do you intend to buy, like last year, or will this year be different?" or "John, I have a question for you. If you bought from me, would this be the first time your company has ever bought this kind of product?" The kind of general response that a question like this elicits can be followed up with more specific questions that would steer the conversation in a more businesslike direction.

A more direct transition can be gotten simply by asking for it directly. "Mary, before I leave here today, I really do have to cover some points," or "There really is something new you need to hear about," and then move into the business side of the call. Another way to focus the dialogue is to use a formal presentation. With this kind of client, I have seen this go two ways. Sometimes the "nice" facade works for you. "Oh, by all means, give me a presentation," but sometimes this kind of client resists formal presentations. If this is the case, simply acknowledge that you have a series of points that you need to make and you can structure a running conversation to cover all these points. Basically, you turn your presentation into a conversation and leave the flip charts in your bag. If you anticipate that this might happen, you might leave the flip charts at home, but put a single sheet of paper on her desk with a series of five points you want to make and then cover them in sequence. The real purpose here of using a formal presentation is to focus the dialogue so that it does not get side-tracked with less businesslike conversation.

2. Bring up objections yourself.

With most clients, this would be a very tricky thing to do. Why would you introduce problems and concerns that may not be on the mind of the client at this time? The problem with this client is that she is probably not making the decisions herself or that she is not capable of acting like a real buyer. After you leave the room this person may go to a superior and say, "Gee, I'd like to buy this product," and the superior will say, "Well, did you ask about this or did you ask about that?" and in essence raise objections that you are no longer in the room to deal with. What you might do is to raise objections and say, "Look, after I leave here, you may have some other concerns about my product, or things that my competitors will raise in my absence. Let me mention a few of the typical ones that might come up and you can tell me whether you think that those are important enough for me to elaborate on." This way you give the client the opportunity to pick and choose among the objections that you can go into without giving her a whole bunch of reasons why she shouldn't buy from you.

3. Handle both sides of the call.

Sometimes clients like this are new to the buying side of the game and really don't know how to play, but ultimately they will be judged on how well they make their purchases. If you are to keep them as clients, you will have to help them to look good while they buy from you. What you can do is throw out a few tips to your client on how to be a tough buyer. You might suggest, "If I were you, I would consider placing your orders during certain times of the year because we offer a better rate," or you might mention that other people in her buying situation behave in certain ways that are to their advantage. I wouldn't give away the store here but if you can throw a few things in their direction to help them be tougher buyers, it might actually work out to your benefit.

4. Stage a gentle "confrontation."

You are on the call and something tells you that this person is not convinced that she is going to buy from you, even though she says she is. With experience, you will get this feeling on calls. You can stage a gentle "confrontation" by expressing this uncomfortable feeling. You might say, "I understand that you will buy from me, and it's not that I don't believe you but I am still concerned that . . ." Here, your concerns should relate to the particulars of the sale. It might be something like not getting a commitment from her company, the money not being in the budget, the company's long-standing relationship with a competitor, or something of the like. Tell her you are concerned, tell her you are worried, tell her you are eager for her business and you don't feel assured that you are getting it; then shut up and let her respond.

5. Get her on your side.

The first thing you have to do is really sell her, really convince her that she should buy your product. Then position yourself as a helper who will help your client get what you are both looking for. If you can convince her that buying your product will make her and her company look good, then even the most insecure buyer can be won over in this fashion. After you get her on your side, here are some thoughts. Try to make it "just you and me." You and I are in this together; how can we work together to convince the people in your organization to buy my product? Ask, "Is there someone else I have to sell?" Ask, "Is there any way I can make you look better in front of your organization?" Ask, "Is there anyone else I can meet with in your organization who can help get this purchase through?"

6. Consider that this person may not be there for long.

I have noticed over the years that the day clients decide they are leaving their job, their behavior toward people who sell them things changes. Tough clients become pussycats. Stand-offish clients become very friendly. The tough objections are gone, but so is the opportunity to make a real sale. Suddenly you are dealing with a client who was tough as nails before, and is now telling you intimate personal details. What happened? It may be that she gave notice last week and will be at this position for only a short while longer. If this sort of thing happens to you, you could go fishing for this possibility by asking your client what her plans might be for next year, or you might ask where she thinks she will be five years from now, personally.

7. Nail down the level of commitment before you leave the room.

That's right. Before you walk out that door, make sure you understand, in very specific terms, just how sold this client is. Here are some approaches to find out.

a. *Ask for the order.* If you are dealing with a product and a buyer, where commitments can be made in real time, you must ask for the order and see whether you get it. If you get anything but a commitment, find out specifically how to go about getting a commitment or what needs to be accomplished before a commitment is made.

b. *Ask about the time line.* OK, this person you are calling on is convinced. How much longer will it take before a commitment can be made? Maybe this person has to meet with a committee. Maybe this person has to get competitive bids. Find out what the time line is to assess just what level of commitment this client is planning for your product.

c. *Find a way to continue the dialogue, even after you have left the room.* Before you leave the room, ask what is next. What do I have to get back to you on? What do you want to hear about? Find out whether there is any way that you can maintain contact in a nonstructured selling situation. If this client is going to be swayed by a competitor, you need to maintain some sort of dialogue with this person, even if it has nothing to do with the particular sale you are trying to make. Get back to her next week about a restaurant she wants to go to, or anything else, but maintain a dialogue—and in passing, ask about the process the sale is going through.

8. Deal with the big surprise when you lose the order.

OK, this one got past you. You thought you had it in the bag and now you find out your client is about to buy from someone else. Here is a step-by-step guide on how to react.

a. *Use any relationship you have as leverage to get details.* First of all, you have to find out what happened, what went wrong, who talked to whom, what got said, what information was shared that persuaded your client to buy somewhere else. Use guilt: "Mary, I'm so surprised. I thought we had a real understanding. I can't believe you would go off and buy from someone else without at least giving me the courtesy of a phone call." Use intimidation: "Frank, I can't believe you didn't give me the opportunity to make a competitive bid for your business. Don't you think it's in the best interest of you and your company to solicit such a thing? I can't imagine that your organization doesn't want to get the best offer possible. Don't you think it's in the best interest of your organization to get competitive bids for any sale it makes? I don't know how this is going to make you look if it comes out that you didn't at least solicit one." Use friendliness: "Chris, I'd really like the opportunity to come in and present the case for my product one more time. I think you know that I won't waste your time and that I could make you look like a real hero by coming away with a superior purchase. What do you say?" Make a scene: "Tom, I can't believe what I'm hearing. My boss is not going to react well to this situation at all and I know that he is going to want to contact someone higher up in your organization. I can't believe you didn't call me when this sale started going this way." Use a more logical approach: "Julie, at least tell me what happened," then listen very carefully to what did happen.

   b. *Never ask, "Is it too late?"* If you're dealing with a client who is skittish on making commitments, the worst thing you can do in a situation like this is to ask whether it's too late. The answer is always yes, because this client will follow the path of least resistance. Just assume that it's not too late and proceed accordingly.

   c. *Get in immediately.* If you are trying to reverse a buying decision, it's been my experience that the longer a buying decision stands unquestioned, the more likely it will stand forever. Hours and days count. A decision that is just made can often be reversed. One that has been around for a few days almost never goes away. Timing is everything, and you have to get in and see the decision maker fast. If you are told, "It is too late and a decision has been made, so don't waste your time coming," insist that you would still like to waste your time anyway. I was once told that a huge contract had expired and that there was no way I could ever get it back. I insisted on making the trip anyway, telling them that I didn't want to talk about my product, rather how my product can be best used and how, in general, people can get the best use out of it. In short, rather than running into a confrontational situation where I was trying to overcome someone's decision, I opted for an end run, played the consultant and tried to raise the argument to another level. I made a trip all the way to Canada, in the dead of winter, to do this. The people at the company were so flattered that I would visit them at a time when they saw very few people from the United States, that I was able to spend a lot of quality time with the person involved. I was able to present different benefits for the use of my product than the client had previously considered. What ended up happening was the entire budget for not just my product, but everyone else's, got increased, and I got back my contract for the next year.

d. *Ask about next time.* If you lost the sale, learn from how the sale went, so that the next round, assuming there is one, will go more to your favor.

Closing Strategies

1. Be direct and ask for specifics.

Simply say, "Can I have the order?" If you get anything but a positive response, doggedly ask for details. What about the time line of the sale? Who else is involved? Whom else do I have to sell? Get specific.

2. If the client tells you that she will buy, ask for clarification.

I know this sounds silly, but sometimes as salespeople, people tell us, "Yes, don't worry, I'll buy from you," and we figure we'll handle the details of how that sale will be executed later on. Don't do it with this client. Ask how soon the order will be placed, in what quantities, and so on.

3. Treat it like a normal sale, once you've gotten to the heart of the selling dialogue.

With this client, once you get past the smoke screen and get into a more businesslike selling dialogue, very often the rest of the call and closing proceeds very much like a normal sale. The trick is getting past the smoke screen.

6

The Client Who Complains About Everything

From the Tough Calls survey:

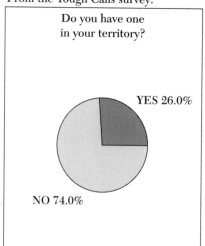

Do you have one
in your territory?

YES 26.0%

NO 74.0%

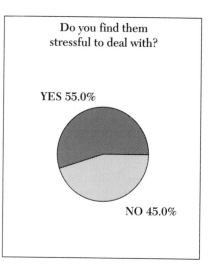

Do you find them
stressful to deal with?

YES 55.0%

NO 45.0%

"Smile, listen, and ask, 'What is the one thing I could do right now to help?'"

Company Manager, research services, Minneapolis, Minn.

All of your clients are going to have some complaints from time to time, but this client complains about everything. Nothing seems good enough and any point you make seems to have a negative side that he will bring out and stick in your face. After a while you dread calling this guy. Every little thing seems to be a tremendous problem.

Pitfalls

1. Agreeing with the complainer about your products and company.

Many complainers whine about your products and will press you to agree with them. It can be tempting. The implication of your agreement is that you get closer to the complainer and the illusion is that you are thus getting closer to making the sale. However, if you agree with him, you validate his negative point of view. You really do have to resist this since agreeing with his relentless complaining devalues the product you sell. I have sold some complainers who are so skilled at their craft that they zoom in on weaknesses in my product and try to get a conversation going about those weaknesses. If you sit around talking about the weak points of your product, you are not getting closer to making a sale.

2. Thinking of this as real complaining.

In your personal life, when someone complains to you about something, he is expressing real emotion to you. But in a business situation where you are trying to sell someone something, complaining is often another way to put you on the defensive and get you to lower your price or give up some kind of concession. Think of business complaining more as posturing for negotiation and less as real complaining.

Selling Strategies

1. Set him up to work for you.

A good complainer can become a terrific resource if you manage him well. This kind of person really does complain about everything. Here's how to put this to good use. Find a tactful, or not so tactful, way to change the subject to your competition. If you can pull this off it can be a terrific way to get competitive reports on the weaknesses of your competitors as told by someone in a buying position. A good complainer can be a fantastic resource to give you ideas on how to sell in a competitive selling environment. Another thing you can do is to redirect the complainer to talking about where he works. If you can get him to start complaining about his coworkers and superiors, again this can be a valuable insight into the politics surrounding this man, and the pressures put on him to buy certain products in certain ways. Often you will have to get to know a complainer for a while before he will complain about your competition and his company. If you can pull off this feat it is well worth the investment of time. Every territory has a few of these complainers. Usually they are dying to tell you all about the weak points of your competition. Complainers can be among your most valuable resources if you manage them properly.

2. Give it back to him in a joking manner.

For many complainers complaints are just a matter of personal style, not policy. Often, if you stick it right back to them when a complaint is issued, you earn their respect. You do have to know your client well before you try this out because if you misjudge it really can backfire.

Complainer:	"I can't believe I just got that last shipment of your product today. Why does it take those guys in your warehouse so long to get this stuff out the door?"
Response:	"Look who's talking! When was the last time you showed up on time for anything? Last time we had lunch you showed up a half hour late."

I know this sounds dumb when I write about it in a book, because you can't see the winks and the nods and the facial expressions that it takes to pull it off. In real life this really can work but, again, you have to know your client well enough to do this.

3. Ask yourself, "What kind of attention does he really want?"

I have sold many complainers who really were not looking for business-related concessions. For these complainers, somehow their heads got wired up into thinking that no one ever listens to them, so they overstate every little thing that bothers them. Selling these complainers is largely about developing a relationship where they feel you are listening to them and taking them seriously. Typically, these clients need a lot more personal attention and less "selling." Here, your job is more to build trust and less to overcome objections. To sell this kind of complainer, try listening more to the feelings behind the complaints, and respond to them. The feelings may sound more like "You didn't hear me" or "You didn't take me seriously."

4. Change your relationship.

As a seller you have no power to change who your client is. If he is a complainer, that is in the nature of who he is and how he presents himself in a buyer-seller relationship. But while you can't change who a complainer is, you can change your relationship with him. Every situation is different, but if you are being pummeled by complaints from this client, stop and think how you are interacting with him and try to fundamentally shift how you act and react with him. If you have been very low-key, try taking a more assertive posture. Some complainers see low-key approaches as weaknesses and throw a lot of complaints at you just to test your metal. If you have been very aggressive, try taking a toned-down approach. While some complainers can sound ferocious, at heart they may be very insecure and your aggressive stance may be intimidating to them on some level, thus causing them to crank up the number of complaints directed at you. The best way to change your relationship, though, is not by changing how you present yourself, but more through empathy and understanding of the complainer's point of view. If you can really reach a point where you understand this person, understand what complaints are real, what complaints are just for posturing, and what complaints are just for personal attention, then you will be in a terrific position to fundamentally change how this client relates to you. Understanding takes time, and in some client relationships you may not have the benefit of a lot of time to do this. Some salespeople can intuitively plug in to these kinds of feelings. It's the kind of thing that comes with experience.

5. Love him.

I have noticed that as you become friends with some complainers, the complaints stop. Sometimes the complaints are just a way of saying, "I haven't bought you yet, and this is my way of keeping you at arm's length and not buying from you." Ignore the complaints and do something personal and friendly. Say, "I hear what you're saying and these are very legitimate complaints. Maybe we can find somewhere to talk about your concerns, over dinner, or find someplace special." You may be surprised at how well a more personal approach gets taken.

6. Separate legitimate complaints from behavior designed to put you on the defensive.

This is the kind of thing that experienced salespeople do strictly on intuition. If you haven't thought about this, consider asking yourself these two questions: First, what does he want to get out of me by acting this way? Is he crazy like a fox, or just crazy? OK, he puts you on the defensive. He makes you crazy by complaining about every little thing. Very often what he really wants is for you to make sure that every little detail of his order gets executed perfectly. He may be a perfectionist who is equally demanding of every little thing that he does in his own work, and this is just getting passed along to you as a natural extension of the way he does things. If this is the case, it is in your best interest to take extra care to make sure that the small details that may be overlooked don't get overlooked in his case. The other possibility is that he is just crazy. Sometimes people whom a company cannot fire, or who have little interpersonal talent, are moved into buying positions. It's no secret that it is much harder to sell than to buy, and very often buyers' jobs are considered positions into which political appointees, family members, or people who cannot be terminated are moved. If this is where this complainer is, and for this reason you may be dealing with a client with no buying authority, check Chapter 4. The second question is: Is this complaint a deal breaker? Remember, after you have sold your product in your territory for a time, you should be able to recognize certain buying patterns that certain kinds of clients have. Does this sound like a real concern, or is it just yet another complaint thrown in your face? Here are a few ways to smoke out real complaints from gratuitous complaints.

a. *You can simply ask.* Ask your client, "I'm glad you brought that to my attention. Is this something you're bringing up because it's important to you, or is this something you're just bringing to my attention for my benefit?"

b. *Ask him to put it in writing.* If you have no idea how serious the complaint might be but you think it might be a big one, ask that person to do some actual work in registering it. It's easy to blow off steam at a salesperson. It's not that much harder to simply sit down and dictate a letter. I've asked about a half dozen clients with these "life or death" sounding complaints to put their concerns in writing to send them on to my boss. Not one of them has ever pursued it further. This also sets up a wonderful dynamic between the client and me. The next time the complaint comes up I simply ask, "Did you ever send that letter to my boss?" Usually the complaint never comes up again.

c. *Ask him whether, if this complaint were resolved, he would buy immediately.* If he says yes and makes you a verbal commitment that if this complaint were resolved he would buy, then you probably have something you should be concerned with. If he hems and haws, and stalls and tries to wiggle out of it, you have just nailed a gratuitous complaint.

7. Minimize the importance of the complaint.

Complainers can be very highly skilled individuals. I have dealt with some who have a rare gift for zooming in on very real weaknesses of the product I'm selling and then pressing me for some kind of confirmation. If they really know their stuff and you really know your stuff, it's very hard to flat out ignore the complaint, or maintain credibility if the complaint is about a legitimate weakness in your product. The best way to handle this is to minimize the weakness; try something like this: "Yes, my product may be a bit larger and bulkier than those of my competitors, but how important do you really think this is in day-to-day use?" You can't really deny that your product has weaknesses, but you can minimize the importance of those weaknesses.

8. Ask yourself whether he is really still upset about something else.

I once had a client who suddenly out of the blue started complaining about everything. At first I started reacting to the complaints themselves. One by one, I would resolve them with time and difficulty. But after a while, I realized that something had changed in our relationship and I couldn't quite put my finger on what it was. Somehow, over the phone, this sort of stuff just never comes out. It wasn't until I took this client out to lunch and we were talking less about business and more about personal things, that this client touched my sleeve and said, "Look, Josh, I have to tell you something that's been on my mind for a while. Remember that last slip-up that occurred three months ago? Well, you gave us a rate break on my next order, but a lot of people I work with felt that you guys got off easy, and since then they've been on my case to be on your case." If you have a good client who suddenly turns into a complainer, stop for a moment and think about what might have transpired in your relationship that might have changed things. Sometimes things that are officially resolved could linger on an emotional level for months afterwards. Here, your job is to play psychoanalyst and get at the feelings that may still be lingering.

9. Ask yourself, "Is he a telephone complainer?"

I have had several clients over the years who are total whiners on the phone, but perfect gentlemen in person. It sounds crazy, but it really is easier to complain to someone over the phone than in person. The phone is less personal and less confrontational. It's easier to make a few negative snaps and hang up. In person, complaining is less easy and, for some clients, their complaints simply disappear when you meet them face to face.

If you are dealing with this particular breed of complainer, make sure that any significant selling points are made face to face. Use the phone only to arrange for visits.

10. If the complaining continues and it's just too relentless, and you feel uncomfortable, try one of these:

a. Ignore the complaints.

b. Acknowledge the complaining and mention that you are being put in a difficult position. Say, "Look, I understand that you are concerned about these things, and it is important for me to hear them and communicate your concerns to the people I work for, but beyond this point you are putting me in an uncomfortable position. I have to professionally represent this company, and I can't compromise my position by agreeing with you or continuing this conversation. I do want your business, but please understand the difficult position you're putting me in."

c. Ask outright not to be included in these discussions. If the complaining persists beyond the point where approach "b" doesn't work, try something more assertive: "I appreciate that you want to share these concerns with me, and that you have done so, but I really can't get involved in these discussions because it compromises my ability to represent the company I work for. I appreciate your bringing these concerns to my attention and I've made note of them, but beyond this point there is nothing more I can do, so if you can leave me out of these discussions in the future I'd appreciate it. Thank you."

d. If the complaints become repetitive, parrot back the complaint, then acknowledge that you have heard it before.

Closing Strategies

Although complainers are often difficult people to live with, they are often easy to close. Very often they have no problem expressing their objections, and if you view their complaints as objections you can use them to close the sale.

1. Say, "I understand that concern you have; if it were resolved, would you buy?"

Then go on to resolve the complaint and close the sale.

2. Shoot the attention to your competitors for a while.

Together complain about every little weakness they have, and then ask for the order for your product.

3. Sift out and come up with the real objections that this client has. Then take them all head-on.

Not only overcome the objections, but bring up peripheral objections that might occur before the complainer has the opportunity to bring them up. In essence you are outcomplaining the complainer. After you have done this, ask for the order. You'll usually get it.

7

The Client Who Says, "It Is Not in the Budget"

From the Tough Calls survey:

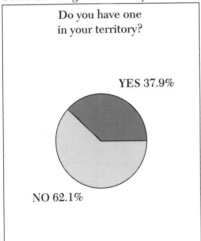

Do you have one in your territory?

YES 37.9%

NO 62.1%

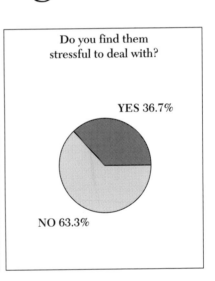

Do you find them stressful to deal with?

YES 36.7%

NO 63.3%

"A lot of effort is put into the project only to have the issue deferred."

Sales and Marketing Manager, broadcast TV hardware, Toronto, Ont.

This client needs little introduction. He introduces himself immediately with those famous words: "Sorry, there is no money in my budget to buy your product." He may be easy to spot, but he is much harder to categorize so that you can deal with him. There are many reasons why there is no money for your project in his budget. To sell him, first you have to find out what kind of no-money client you are dealing with. Once the no-money objection is raised, your client may think that his job of dealing with you is over. In reality your job of dealing with him is just beginning.

Pitfalls

1. Taking the "no money in the budget" objection at face value.

In my experience only about 20 percent of the people who give you the no-money-in-the-budget line are really telling you that the budget is spent for this year and the next year. Most are really expressing different objections, and the reasons that there is no money for your product can vary tremendously. When you are told that there is no money, stop whatever you are doing and start asking some questions to reassess your situation. Here are four questions to ask that can steer you to different ways to handle this objection:

a. *Ask your client, "Do you currently buy the product I sell from someone else?"* If your client says yes, then the deeper issue has nothing to do with budgets. Get it? Right now there is no money in the budget for your product, as opposed to the product of your competition. Here, your job is to do a competitive selling job to get monies allocated for your product over someone else's. See Chapter 10.

b. *Ask your client, "What do I have to do to convince you to give my product a try?"* If he comes back at you with some talk about "work with me to get a price to give you a try," then the deeper issue may have less to do with budgets and more to do with coming up with the right deal. Here, the no-money objection really is a negotiation tactic to get a better price. See the discussion of the Price Grinder in Chapter 1.

c. *Ask your client, "How do you see my product fitting into the future of your business?"* or *"Are you planning to buy this kind of prod-*

uct in the future?" If he really does not see a future, then he is not sold on the benefits of buying your product. This has nothing to do with budgets. He is not sold on your product. Ask some more questions to find out whether your product and his needs really are a match. Go back to square one and start selling your product, all over again.

d. *Ask yourself, "Can this company really afford what I am selling?"* Often when you are prospecting you come across accounts that you mistake for real prospects. Sometimes when they say they have no money it really is because they have no money or because they have no need for your product. Again, it's not about budgets, its about company size and need. Sometimes you can waste a lot of time on clients like this because they don't tell you they are just too small to buy your product.

2. *Offering a rate concession when you hear there is no money in the budget.*

As I mentioned above, there are a lot of reasons why you might be hearing the no-money objection. It may be about getting a rate concession, but it may not be. The problem is that once you offer a rate concession your client may expect it whether he would have bought without it or not. Ask yourself, is this more about cost or more about timing? It could be about both, but if it is more about timing you could be cheapening your hand by bringing up a rate concession too soon. It is better to wait and first find out what kind of no-money account you are dealing with.

3. *Trying a prestige sell.*

Sometimes when you hear the no-money objection, you are calling on a client who has true Bean Counter tendencies. For him, the no-money objection is a convenient, all-inclusive, financially oriented objection. If he really is a Bean Counter, the prestige sell typically is a real turnoff. For many clients, buying the best of the best is desirable, but if you are calling on a Bean Counter, he will want to know more about the nuts and bolts and the bottom line, and less about your company's fabulous image.

I am not selling something that is going to cost you money, I am selling you something that will make you money!

Selling Strategies

1. Position your product as a financial benefit.

If your prices are lower than those of your competitors, then the financial case is easy to demonstrate. You might take out a pad of paper and show him, with real numbers, just how much money he will save by buying from you. But what if your product is not the cheapest? With this client, you may still have to present the unique features of your product in financial terms.

- If your product does something faster, write up a typical situation demonstrating how much money gets saved with the faster application your product will provide.
- If your product is of higher quality, and therefore lasts longer, work out the numbers to show just how much money a longer-lasting product might save.
- If your product is "future proved" to adapt to evolving technologies, ask how much it would cost to have to up-grade to an entirely different technology in the future.
- If your product presents a new potential revenue source, work out the numbers to show just how much.

2. Define and work the time line.

If part of this objection is really about timing, then you must find out what the timing really is. Ask, "When will you get next year's budget?" or "When will you begin to plan for next year's budget?" Once you know when he gets his money, plan backward from there. Consider that when there is money to be spent, your competitors will be clamoring for the budget just like you. It's better to get your major selling points in ahead of the crowd. If you have not gotten business from this client before, consider that your competitors have had a whole year to reinforce their presence. Also, when the budget is handed to your buyer, he may have a lot of other decisions to make simultaneously. You could be lost in the crowd. Just showing up at the party at the right time does not mean you'll be asked to dance.

3. Ask for a test.

It may well be that the next budget cycle is six months away, but why don't you ask, "Is there some incremental money available for a test?" Tell him you understand that there is no money now, but that when there is money and budgets need to be allocated for next year, how will he make a good decision with regard to your product? If your product is as good as you say, his company could benefit tremendously. Why not spend a little bit of money now for a test?

4. Help your client find the money.

Once you have sold your client on the value of your product, if you present yourself properly you may be in a position to help him find the money. Here you take a less pressured, soft sell approach and act as a consultative salesperson. A hard sell will not get you into these kinds of discussions because the client will not give you access to the working details of his business. It is very hard to establish this kind of working relationship with a buyer. You have to get to know your client's business, establish real trust, and develop a rapport where your client depends on you or at least considers your input valuable. If you can develop this kind of relationship, you can ask the following questions. "Can the budget for my product type be increased?" You might ask him what kind of information you can provide that can get the budget for your type of product increased overall. Here, stories about how other companies have successfully utilized your product for other applications might be helpful.

- Ask, toward the end of the year, "Is there any unspent money?"
- Ask, "Can money for my product come out of a different budget?" Here, if you know your client's business well enough, you can reallocate some of his funds.
- Ask, "Can money for my product come out of money budgeted for a similar product from a competitor?" Here you might refer to Chapter 10 again.
- Ask, "Is there any money you can save elsewhere that could be spent on my product?" Here, again, you really do have to know your client's business on a level of detail.

- Ask, "Can we bill you later?" If this sale is really being held up by timing, then see whether you can work with your client on a later billing scheme. If it's toward the end of his company's fiscal year, and the company you work for can accept a late bill, then see if he will buy ahead of next year's budget approval.

5. Offer a guarantee involving money.

If there is any hesitancy about buying your product because the client is not sold on it, then offering a financially oriented guarantee is often helpful. If this client really watches the budget carefully, then if you offer a purchase that will not cost anything if it is not successful, he is more likely to go along with it.

6. Consider the psychology of calling on a Bean Counter.

The client who is a Bean Counter is a unique psychological study. He looks as if he was sent over from central casting to play an accountant and ended up as your client instead. Here are some of my thoughts:

a. *Prepare for a no-nonsense call.* This is less about relationships and more about the bottom line. Keep chit-chat to a minimum and put your personality on hold and get to the meat of what you want to talk about quickly.

I've found that Bean Counters are very concrete thinkers. Selling them an abstract concept is nearly impossible. Often the psychology of such clients is that they react very favorably to products or proposals that *save* them money. It is harder to sell them on products that can *make* them money. Bean Counters have an easy time picturing the here and now: "This is what my spreadsheet looks like right now. If I shave 10 percent off right here, what does it look like?" They have a much harder time picturing what it would be like next year if your product were implemented and an unpredictable amount of increased revenues came in. Make your call concrete. If you have a product that can be demonstrated, do so.

[handwritten margin note:] almost all of my clients

Closing Strategies

1. Put it in terms of the money.

It's the language they will understand. It's all about money. Two simple approaches work best here: a) how we will save you money, or b) how we will make you more money.

2. Put the numbers in writing.

Write up your proposal from the bottom line. Show them in real terms how much financial benefit is involved. Show them, "This is exactly what buying my product will cost" and "This is the financial benefit," then directly ask for the order. Typical response, "Well, we will want to look at the numbers, but if they look OK we will have a deal."

8

The Client Who
Is Indecisive

From the Tough Calls survey:

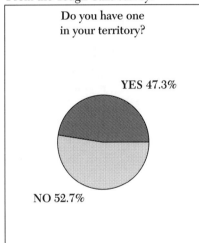

Do you have one
in your territory?

YES 47.3%

NO 52.7%

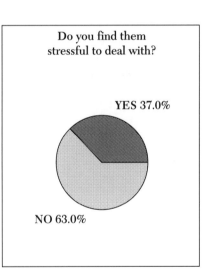

Do you find them
stressful to deal with?

YES 37.0%

NO 63.0%

*"Find out if the new and different is tormenting them. Also, find
out if he/she is afraid of losing their job in an era of down sizing."*
Marketing Manager, on-line service, New York, N.Y.

Decisions can be scary. A buying decision is a highly visible employee behavior that can be evaluated in her next performance
review.

Decisions can be boring. If staff is short and things are extremely busy and the decision can be put off, it probably will be
and no one will be interested in resurrecting it.

Decisions can be unpopular. If there are several people involved in a buying decision who do not get along, resolving internal conflict can be very unpleasant.

The indecisive client is frustrating to deal with and can waste valuable time. Sometimes it is easier to deal with an outright negative decision. If the answer is no, ask why not and decide whether to fight another day or move on to a client with more potential, but the indecisive client's situation just goes on and on and does not resolve itself. Your job is to help it resolve.

Pitfalls

1. Pushing when there is clear resistance.

Pushing for the order is what you are hired to do, but with some indecisive clients, the harder you push, the harder they will resist. Beyond a point this becomes unproductive for you because you can push yourself right out of consideration. At some point you have to sense that you are dealing with an indecisive client and stop to reevaluate. Before you can eliminate resistance, you have to find out why it exists. Stop pushing and start asking questions.

2. Not reading the objections emotionally.

After you have sold your product a while, you should know which objections point to real product concerns and which are just fear or insecurity coming to the surface. If your client keeps throwing anxiety-type objections at you, listen and respond to the feelings. Say, "Look, I know your concern, but thousands of people have bought this product before with no problems. I'm sure your case will be no different."

3. Losing patience.

It's easy to throw up your hands and say, "This person doesn't know anything and I have to talk her into everything she should be doing all along. I have to do her job for her." Be patient; sometimes working with an indecisive client means starting the sales dialogue at a much more basic point than you are used to. Remember, she may be indecisive, but she is the client and just because she takes a long time to make up her mind does not mean she will not buy your product or will not buy it from someone else given the proper attention.

Selling Strategies

1. Give her a deadline to buy.

I have one very good client who has never bought anything from me unless there was a crisis or a deadline. This company is understaffed, and people are most often reacting to crisis, not planning their moves. Using deadlines is familiar to us all. Come up with a desired benefit like a discount, an extra service, an extra upgrade, a sample of a new product, and so on. Then tell your client that she can get it only if she buys by a certain date. Sometimes your direct contact on an account appreciates your setting a deadline because she can go and use it internally to help get others motivated to make a decision. I have been involved with sales situations where the actual incentive offered for a deadline was really quite small. It's the psychological impact of hearing that word: deadline.

2. Use competitive pressure.

There are many clients who watch their competitors more carefully than their customers. Sometimes you can get an account like this to buy just to block a competitor from buying. Come up with a buy specific to your product where there is limited availability (only so much product, just so much capacity, only so much room on this batch, only one magazine back cover, only five left of the older design that we are heavily discounting, and so on), then tell your client that there is only so much left and she can have the right of first refusal to buy it until next Tuesday. After next Tuesday anyone can buy it, and of course "anyone" could be a direct competitor.

3. Sell the idea that a specific sale is a given.

If this client hates making buying decisions, this approach often works because it eliminates the need for anyone to make a decision. If you can get an indecisive client into a pattern of buying at a certain time from you, sometimes the momentum of that pattern can close a sale for you. Step back and think how your client buys over the course of the year. Is there a time you can get your client to buy from you consistently year after year, season after season? Every product is different, but if you sell school supplies it might be in anticipation of the opening of the school year. If you sell cold remedies it might be at the start of winter. Next year, instead of going in for that one purchase, sell her on the idea that she really should buy from you at this time every year. See whether you can get her to agree that buying at this time should be a given. If it becomes a given in your client's mind, no buying decision needs to be made for you to get that order. Once you get that one given sale nailed down in the client's mind every year, start working on a second given sale, then a third, and so on.

4. Start asking for an order six months in advance.

It seems to take forever for some indecisive clients to make up their minds. That's fine if you plan ahead and give them a long time to do it. Take a step back and point out the advantages of buying from you at different times and ask them when they might be more likely to buy. Focus in on times that are a few months off. As the months tick by, call every month to remind them that the time is approaching. This gives the indecisive client time to get used to the idea of buying.

5. Ask for an even bigger order that redefines the buying formula.

If it's hard to get someone to consider small purchases, is it crazy to ask for a big one? Sometimes with an indecisive buyer, it is actually easier to get a big order through than a small one. The reason is that a big order will have to have the input of other people in the organization, while smaller purchases may be controlled by just your indecisive client. This is far easier to write about than to do. I once was able to make just this kind of sale. I was dealing with an indecisive client who would buy from me sporadically. He clearly had a lot of anxiety about making any purchase, and it was clear that he had to get others in his organization to sign off every time he had to place a single order. On my next call with him, I leveled with him and asked whether he was as frustrated with the situation as I was. Of course he was. Here he was powerless to do anything more than run back and forth among different people and recommend sporadic purchases. It was a tremendous waste of his time. Working with him, I was able to set up a group meeting with five other people in his company, including all the department heads who would be involved with these kinds of purchases. After the presentation I asked for a contract with specific times when orders would be placed. When I got this order, my frustrated client was as happy about it as I was.

6. See the client in person.

I had a client who could not make up his mind to buy anything over the phone, but every time I would see him in person he would buy something from me. Once I was going in to try to sell him a large program that would take months to work through and had no intention of selling him on a small purchase, but toward the end of my big-picture presentation he pulled out a mailing I had done a few days before, and bought the tiniest ad anyone could have ever imagined. There really is something about being there that helps people make up their minds. If you have trouble getting in to see a client, reread Chapter 2.

7. Address client insecurity.

An insecure client is usually an indecisive client. According to Jim Wattenmaker, President of Wattenmaker Advertising, insecure clients need far more attention than regular clients. "You have to martial far more information and persuasive material than would ordinarily be needed; you really have to overpower them with so much information that making a decision becomes much easier." It's not just a case of psychology; it can also be a question of timing, says Wattenmaker. "There are times when every client is insecure—he could be coming off a terrible fourth quarter and the climate at his organization may be very down. Sometimes the same idea or product that will not sell in this kind of climate will sell immediately when things warm up."

Finally, Wattenmaker suggests that believing in your product and being willing to lay it on the line can make the difference. If your client believes that you will risk everything, he may just go along. Wattenmaker once got his agency the order to produce a major sales meeting. His direct contact could not sign off on the project without the approval of others in his organization, so the client set up a group meeting including the president of the whole company. After Wattenmaker's presentation there was dead silence in the room. All eyes eventually turned to the company president. The president looked up at Wattenmaker and said, "All right, Jim, but you know your neck is on the line with this one." This was the defining moment at which Jim either laid his neck on the line or did not. Someone who didn't believe in his product might have softened his position. Jim didn't back down, and he made the sale. If your clients act insecure, make them feel you're a true believer who will back them to the hilt.

8. *Ask yourself, "Is she waiting for me to offer her a deal?"*

Some clients use the front of being indecisive as a way to get you to lower your price. They'll tell you they just can't make up their mind, they just don't know what to do, when all along they are basically sitting in wait for you to come down in price. The tricky thing is that some of these people will not tell you this is what they want; you almost have to figure it out through mind reading. I was once involved in a selling situation where a buyer had all kinds of product objections. We were involved in some very elaborate discussions that went on for literally hours. At some time the discussion of the benefits of my product versus another bordered on the philosophical. I kept my manager apprised of the progress of these discussions, thinking that he would be very impressed that I was able to hold my own at the depth of detail required. Ultimately, the detail meant nothing. After hours and hours of debate and entertaining, finally my manager said, "Josh, look, you're wasting far too much time on this client. Why don't you just try cutting her a deal?" I called up the client and it was as if no time had passed. She immediately regained her footing and reslammed right back into the selling dialogue almost at the exact sentence where we had left off a week before. Then I said, "Wait a minute, I have whole different approach I want to try." I offered a deal and it was accepted on the spot. I was in shock. Sometimes clients who really want a deal feel too embarrassed to ask for one directly. A lot of the indecision is just posturing. If you suspect this is the kind of client you are dealing with, check out Chapter 1.

9. Ask yourself whether it's your client or is it where she works.

Sometimes the indecision you are dealing with is not the indecision of your client contact, but the indecision of the organization that she has to interact with to get a buying decision made. For help with this client, see Chapter 4.

10. Ask her, "Is the answer really no, but you won't tell me?"

If you really feel that the dialogue is going absolutely nowhere, this can be a showstopper. If she tells you that the answer really is no, at least you got your answer and you can stop wasting time on this account. If she bristles at the question and is taken aback by it, sometimes you can use this reaction to get her to move closer to buying.

Closing Strategies

Closing indecisive clients is what dealing with them is all about. You have to do all the basics of selling correctly, but getting a commitment always takes an extra effort.

1. Prepare, prepare, prepare for one massive close.

First of all, try to do the close in person if you can. Then work with your management before you go into that room and know just how far you can go with every parameter. Anticipate any concession you might have to make and get approval to grant it beforehand. Also be prepared to remind your client about every selling point you have ever made with her. Before you go into that room think through every objection she has ever expressed to you and think about whether you have satisfied it. You must close her in that face-to-face meeting. If she waffles and walks out without giving you the order, she may be gone forever.

2. Ask, "Do you want a blue one or a green one?"

This is the old closing technique where instead of asking the client whether she wants to buy or not, you ask her which one of two different varieties of the product you are selling she wants to buy. This kind of closing technique was very popular in the 1950s, and today I think clients are just too smart for it, but for the indecisive client, bring this old technique out of mothballs and use it. It may be techniquey, it may be transparent, it may be obvious, but sometimes indecisive clients almost like to be manipulated into a sale. On some crazy level, psychologically it might feel as if they are getting off the hook.

3. Close with an "obvious choice" presentation.

If you are in a market leadership position, try this. Make a column list of every reason someone in your client's position would buy your kind of product. Your list might read Product Quality, Company Longevity, Pricing, Customer Service, Product History, and so on. If your product is technical, include a list of specs or features. Then in side-by-side columns across from each category list all of your and your chief competitors' features and parameters. Walk your client through this list line by line, pointing out how your product is the obvious choice every time. If your client is with you as you go line by line, at the end ask for the order. Tell her she has to buy from you since it is the obvious choice.

4. Tell her no.

I am usually more of a soft sell, but for this one client I behaved way out of character. I held up my hands like a crossing guard and said, "Wait a minute, you just can't do this! We've worked out all the details, we've talked about all the different options, and you told me this is what you wanted. We just can't go back to square one." I got agitated and emotional. My client backed down, reconsidered another stall, and bought. Sometimes you just have to get emotional and take a stand.

5. Entertain personally and ask for the order.

Indecisive clients need the feeling that you will back them up personally. Sometimes personal entertainment soothes this sort of anxiety. The old adage of asking for the order as you are in the middle of paying the check works with some clients, but I think it's more of the case of making a more personal commitment and then asking for the order.

6. Close soft.

Build trust and then ask for the order. If they feel you will take care of them no matter what, clients will be more likely to buy what you are selling. Take your selling dialogue step by step. Emphasize that you have been very patient with them and have helped them every step of the way. Gently remind them that you have had to work out many small details that took extra effort on your part. Remind them that you have been with them throughout this selling dialogue—and then ask for the order.

7. Close hard.

Generate pressure using some of the techniques above, then ask for the order. Some indecisive clients really need a hard close. They almost feel relieved when you do this. It is as if you are making the decision for them. One approach that works well is to use the "fear and greed close" detailed in Chapter 19.

9

The Client Who
May Cancel the Order

From the Tough Calls survey:

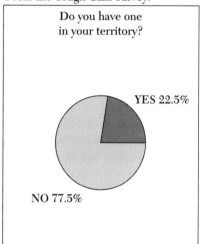

Do you have one
in your territory?

YES 22.5%

NO 77.5%

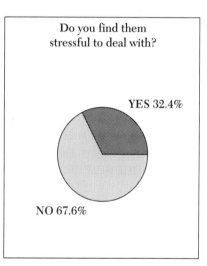

Do you find them
stressful to deal with?

YES 32.4%

NO 67.6%

"Any of my clients could call me up and cancel their contract. It keeps me up at night."

Research Consultant, New York, N.Y.

It was a tough competitive fight, but after several meetings I managed to get my competition dumped and negotiate a large contract increase that would start at the beginning of the following year. It was a major coup and represented the biggest commitment this company had ever made to us. When January came and the big contract started to roll, we were pumped. A month later the company president was pushed out and a new president came in who immediately pronounced the company to be a financial disaster. Draconian budget slashing began, the company was completely restructured, and 25 percent of the entire staff was laid off. A relatively small detail of all this carnage was that my contract was canceled.

This may be the kind of scenario that keeps salespeople up at night worrying about their territories. It shouldn't. Most sales are lost not because of business restructuring, but because of neglect. Most sold business goes not with a bang, but a whimper. It really is much more fun to make a new sale than to maintain or build on current business. I struggle with this every day. It doesn't help that the people you report to are probably far more impressed when you bring in new business than when you tell them about the terrific job you have been doing to maintain existing business. As salespeople, we can sometimes get carried away and forget our current customer base. At the heart of the problem is that things change. At the time you made the sale, you worked through the objections, concessions, and pricing. Your client evaluated competitive bids for the product you sell, but a week or a year later, any of these things may have changed, and the concessions that once cinched the deal may be far less valuable.

Pitfalls

1. Letting the romance get stale.

You have been trying to get their business, pursuing them, visiting them, romancing them, haggling with them, lunching with them, building a relationship with them; then you get the big order and they don't hear from you. How does it look to them? "Love 'em and leave 'em" does not go over well with clients.

2. Assuming that since the client has signed a contract, the business is a given.

Contracts don't seem to mean as much today as they once did. Ten years ago a contract really meant something; today many companies have reevaluated what a buying commitment really is. I think of a contract as an "intent to buy" as opposed to a done deal. The underlying commitment to a contract has more to do with the perception of value a client places on your product and company. If that goes out the window, the written contract will eventually go too.

3. *Being too much of a gentleman or gentlewoman to talk about your competition.*

In my travels I have met some old-timers who talk about the good old days of selling when your job was to "sell your own product" and not talk about your competition. Those days are gone. You have to assume that your competitors are trying to steal your business. Isn't that what you're trying to do to them? If you don't monitor your competition, you could get blindsided if they start to make successful competitive advances.

4. *Assuming that since the client has started to buy, he does not still need to be sold.*

You live your product; the client only buys it. It is easy to forget that he may simply forget why he bought your product in the first place. I have called on people who have forgotten key features of my product year after year, even though they are currently buying it.

Selling Strategies

1. *Keep the romance alive.*

Many salespeople, including myself, are motivated by "the thrill of the kill" that winning new business brings, but in many territories the biggest gains are made by increasing existing business. It's easy for me to tell you that you should spend extra time romancing the business you already have, but the practical side of maintaining a romance is more about time than sincerity. Where does the time to do all this come from? When you have to prioritize how much time you spend building new business versus keeping existing business, what gets left out? Sometimes being objective here is harder than it looks. It's easy to understand how much revenue a new account will generate. Something over zero is always a gain. The opportunities that exist with your current client base may be more subtle to discover.

Here are some other thoughts on maintaining the romance:

a. *Work out tricky details during the honeymoon.* When you first make a sale, there is a romance period that lasts for a while. The client has not only bought your product, he has bought you. No client likes to think he made a bad decision, so at the point of the sale when your client thinks you can do no wrong, work out any difficult details that you think might come out later.

b. *Use personal entertainment.* Boating, ballet, baseball, golf, or dinner, we all know it works.

c. *Contact the client and don't sell anything.* A service contact sends the message "you are more than just another order." Call to see whether his first order was handled correctly or showed up on time, or to give him a tip on using his new product that he may have not thought of before. Send a letter thanking him for becoming a new client. Let him know that this is a service call and you're not trying to sell him anything.

d. *Send handwritten notes.* If telling him you care is about managing your time, this is one of the most time effective ways to make this statement. Send him an article, send him a note, write him a personal message on a Christmas card.

2. Don't stop selling.

When I started working with Ann Belle Rosenberg of *Video Systems* magazine, I was almost embarrassed when we would go on joint presentations to good loyal clients. She would give them a hard sell as if they were only buying from her competition. Sometimes the people in the room would wink at me and smile as if to say, "There goes crazy Ann Belle, you would think I never bought anything from her in my life." But the people doing the winking were not seeing what Ann Belle could see coming. Over the course of a few years I noticed that her contracts seemed to stick where others, including some of my own, did not. It did not matter that the people in the room were already sold. By overselling, Ann Belle made her contracts stick through personnel changes, budget cuts, industry downsizings, and corporate buyouts. It may seem crazy to be sitting in a room full of people who are sold on your product and sell them all over again, but it's only crazy like a fox.

3. Monitor your competition.

When you are pursuing a client, you have license to make hard competitive sales presentations. But I find that once you are getting business from a client, he is often less tolerant of hard competitive selling. From the seller's point of view this makes no sense: Before he was buying from you, you had no business to lose from a competitor making advances on your ground. Now that you are getting business from this client, you have plenty to lose from a direct competitor. But when you have some business from a client, you have an inside track that is an ongoing dialogue with the client. Defensive selling means using your ongoing relationship as leverage to keep competitors out.

The essence of defensive selling is to routinely (and subtly) monitor the feelings of your client regarding your competition. You need to find ways to bring up your competitors in passing conversation to see whether they are making progress in stealing your business. Talking about a competitor should never be the central focus of any visit, however. If you spend more time talking about your competition than your product, you may indirectly be selling for your competition. The best time to monitor your competition is when defenses are down and time pressure is off. Social face-to-face meetings like lunch are ideal.

Here are several approaches:

- With humor: "Is all that stuff my competition is saying about me starting to make any sense to you?"
- Questioning your way into the back door: "How is my product doing for you? How could my product be improved? How does it compare with what others are offering you?"
- More direct: "Can I have your assurance that my business with you will continue? Will you be giving any business to my competition?"

- If you find a competitor is making headway, you can deal with it the same way you would in any competitive selling situation.

4. Sell defensively.

If you are watching your competitors in your territory, then you will hear that they are coming up with a new feature or pricing strategy, or a new product, or a new service enhancement, or something that will offer competitive value to what they are selling. The next time you speak with a client, you can bring up the product feature and ask whether your client views it as important. You do not have to mention the fact that your competition has this feature; if your client does not already know about it there is no point in telling him. If you can keep the conversation in the abstract, defenses will be lower. You might offer some ideas as to why this feature is not as valuable as many might think it is, or that your organization is working on a similar feature and will have it out in three months. If you have the inside track and can discuss this feature with your client before your competition does, you will plant a defensive barrier that protects your business.

5. Check for romance decay.

You are very busy and think you have spent enough time with a client, but you can't know every detail of every one of your clients, and it's easy to misjudge some situations. Here are some warning signs that your romance with your client may be going into decay.

   a. *You are given no details.* When you ask about future business, no details are volunteered. Does he not have the details, or does he not want to share them with you because they will reveal some bad news?
   b. *It's harder to get through on the telephone.* Is he just too busy, or is he just too busy to talk to you?
   c. *There's a change in your client's tone when you do get him on the phone.* Does your client sound as if your phone call is an opportunity or an inconvenience?

d. *He does not have time for a visit.* Does he not have time to see you, or is he just not making the time available?

e. *You are told, "Don't worry."* When I hear "Don't worry" from a client I respect and trust, I take it at face value, but when I hear this from someone I do not know, I panic. Sometimes "Don't worry" is shorthand for "Get lost! I am going to make up my own mind about this purchase, and since you probably are not going to be part of it, I don't want to waste my time dealing with you right now, so don't worry." If you think things are going sour with a client, it's best to get in to see him face to face as quickly as you can. Face to face is where the deeper objections come out and where you can have the best chance of turning around a perception that is going bad.

6. Be a healthy sales paranoiac.

Sales stars are always running a little scared. On the surface they give the typical "positive attitude" front that they are so well trained to project. But underneath the surface they worry. When I hire salespeople I look for this quality. It means they will anticipate problems rather than get hit with them as they come up.

7. Start a tradition.

If you are in a long-term selling business, start a tradition around a holiday or special time of the year that comes just before business is to be renewed: a New Year's concert, the first golf outing in early spring, a pre-Thanksgiving dinner at a favorite restaurant, a warm-up lunch before negotiating a contract. Ann Belle Rosenberg hosted a dinner on the second night of a major industry trade show. The group was called the Video Club and met year after year. It became such a regular event that at one point the regular members were actually given membership cards and old members who had moved on into different positions in their respective companies would sometimes show up to visit old friends.

8. Say thank you.

If a client spends $2,000 with you, you may think that he is a small client, that he is getting a good product for a fair price, and that that is reward enough, but on some emotional level that client might think, "I just gave this person $2,000 and he didn't say thank you." It may not be his money, but it is money that he controls and may feel emotionally connected to. In your personal life, if someone walked up to you and gave you $2,000, you would say thank you. Take him out to a thank-you lunch, send him a thank-you card, send flowers, or just remember to say those words, but forgetting them can send a negative emotional message.

Closing Strategies

1. Sell up. The best defense is an offense.

When you ask for a bigger order, hidden objections will come to the surface. If there was ever a problem of your losing your business, it will come up and you can deal with it.

2. Get a verbal commitment for anticipated business.

Although it may be premature to get an order before budgets are set and so on, getting personal assurance will emotionally commit that client to being your advocate. When your client and his boss or other buying influences go into that closed-door session where buying decisions are made, that client will be motivated to fight harder for you if he has made a personal commitment to you. No one wants to come out and say, "Look, I know what I told you, but my boss cut the budget to pieces and there was just nothing I could do about it." Aside from being personally embarrassing, it shows a lack of power. Another kind of commitment to ask for is that your client look out for your purchase as it flows through the company. Ask, "If it looks as if the buy for my product is in jeopardy, will you let me know in time so that I can respond constructively?"

3. *Close your way up the food chain.*

If you want a target for your continued selling efforts, ask this question: "When it comes to buying the product I sell, who is your top supplier?" If you're not at the top, you have some selling insurance to do. Your client may be buying now, but what if there is a budget cut? Selling your way up to the top now will protect your business from the inevitable.

10

The Client Who Buys Elsewhere: Likes a Competitive Product

From the Tough Calls survey:

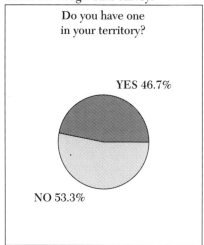

Do you have one in your territory?

YES 46.7%

NO 53.3%

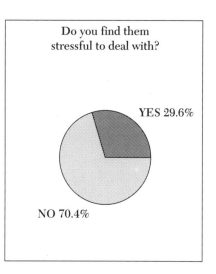

Do you find them stressful to deal with?

YES 29.6%

NO 70.4%

"They are not willing to try a new proven method even if it means improvement, but rather prefer to stay with the old one."

Owner/"Cheerleader," financial services company,
San Antonio, Texas

Your client needs your product but is buying a similar product from someone else. You tell her your product is better. She says you are wasting your time because she is satisfied with the product she is now buying. "Why change?" she asks you. The temptation is to go for the throat and totally trash the competitor's product to try to get her business. Although it may be gratifying to feel that you have fought the good fight, this plan can backfire. If the person you are calling on made the buying decision on your competitor's product, slamming that product not only questions the product, it questions the judgment of the person who bought it.

But clients do not dislike all forms of competitive selling. Clients need competitive information to help them evaluate competitive products. If you don't tell them the weak points of your competitor's product, who will? Smart buyers who respect you will often ask your opinion of your competitors.

The first step in selling against an established product purchase is to find out why the client bought that product in the first place. But when you ask why, you will often get logical answers that don't always give you insight into the more emotional motivations that went into her initial purchase. Sometimes digging out the emotional side of the buy is a real investigation.

Pitfalls

1. Putting your client on the defensive.

When a client makes a buying decision, she has committed herself emotionally to that product. Even if there is little emotional commitment to the decision, the organization she works for will evaluate her on this and other purchasing decisions she makes. No matter how you look at it, if she bought the product, she "owns" that buy. If it comes out that it was a bad buying decision, it will make her look bad. I have seen so many salespeople walk into a call and announce that buying from their competitor was a bad idea, trash the product, and show reasons to buy their own product. Even if you are very persuasive, your chances for success are slim. You will more likely accomplish three things. First, you will immediately launch your client's mind into a mode where she is sitting there thinking about even more reasons why she made the right decision in the first place. If you overcome every objection while you are sitting in the room, she may go home that night, talk to her husband, and come back at you with three more objections. Losing this kind of fight means losing face for your client, either to herself or to the organization where she works. Second, you will lose a chance to probe in a conversation where defenses are down for deeper, possibly more emotional reasons why the buy went the way it did. Third, you will possibly turn her off to listening to you in the future. It may feel good to trash the competition, but I say don't do it. Bite your tongue if you have to; kick yourself under the desk if you have to. When you trash the competition you are not acting in your own best interest.

2. Bounding into a competitive presentation before you know exactly why she is buying a competitive product.

There are reasons she is not buying from you. If she does not understand your product, it may be because her perceptions are based on a superficial misunderstanding. If your knee-jerk reaction is to go into a canned pitch, you could be reinforcing the same superficial perceptions that are keeping her away.

Selling Strategies

1. Give a comparative, not competitive, presentation.

The way to make an unsolicited attack effective is to make it more like a comparison of all competitive products and not just a head-to-head attack on the competitor who now is getting the business. Comparative selling means selling with side-by-side facts or ideas; our numbers compared with their numbers, our specs compared with their specs, our position compared with their position, our track record compared with their track record, our survey results compared with their survey results. Let the facts do the attacking, not you. Even though your ultimate discussion may skew toward you versus the people who now get the business, your initial presentation will talk more about the big picture, and you will be inviting comment on a higher level as opposed to a one-on-one attack. Since this global way to present your case does not directly attack the product your client bought, defenses should be lower. If done well, a comparative presentation presents information that will help your client understand more about the strengths and weaknesses of all products in your category. The inevitable outcome of starting a presentation like this is that your client will want to know how your product stacks up against the product she is now buying. My experience is that you really don't have to push this side of the discussion; it's just the logical outcome of you sitting in a room with someone who is buying from someone else when you make this kind of presentation.

2. Attack on a theoretical level.

By shifting your attack to a more abstract level, sometimes you can sidestep the client's ego long enough to sell her.

If you represent a national chain of stationery stores and are trying to get business from a client who has been buying from a local stationery store for the past ten years, it may be a very emotionally difficult sell. Here going abstract is a good idea. Talk about the value of buying from a larger chain, any larger chain. Talk about the benefits of multi-store buying and how that benefits the client you're trying to sell. Talk about the credit terms that a national chain can offer versus a smaller local supplier. Here you are not talking about just your company, you're talking about any national chain versus any local supplier. Keep your company and the mom-and-pop store out of the conversation at first. Win your points in the abstract, then bring your product and your competition into the dialogue. If you have your dialogue focused on the real-world players up front, your client may be sitting there, worrying that if she buys from you, someday she will have to tell the people she has had a long-standing relationship with that they're not getting her business. By keeping the discussion out of the emotional real world, often you can win your points. One cautionary note: A lot of clients I have called on are not abstract thinkers and really do need a nuts-and-bolts approach. Sometimes trying to sell nuts-and-bolts clients in an abstract way fizzles.

3. Differentiate your product.

Differentiating means documenting the details of how your product is different than products you compete with. Before you can prove that your product is better, you have to prove that it is different. You live with your product all day long, but your client only buys it. It is very possible that your client thinks of your product and those of your competitors as being pretty much the same. Sometimes investing in an entire call just to differentiate your product is important. I once made a call on a large client and spent the entire time just pointing out the honest differences between my product and the products I compete with. We kept the discussions focused on just that, and instead of asking for the order in the form of a sale, I asked for the order in the form of my client's agreement that the products I was competing with were fundamentally different. I left the client's office satisfied that I had made the first step of the sale. I did this by offering a nonjudgmental side-by-side, feature-by-feature list of differences. I did not get into discussions of how these differences proved better or worse. If the conversation started heading in that direction, I refocused and restated my initial intent on making the call, which was not to prove which product was better, just to prove how they were different. On my next visit to that client I started by saying, "During my last visit we agreed that my product was different than the product you are now buying and other products that I compete with. Here are reasons why my product will benefit your company more, and here is what you are missing by not buying it." I went on to win the sale. For more information on differentiating your product, review Chapter 1.

4. Get her more excited about your product.

I've read too many books on selling that say that if you are enthusiastic about your product, your client will also get enthusiastic about your product. Your own enthusiasm is a great start, but it is rarely enough. In sales our personal enthusiasm is a given. If you don't have it for the product you sell, you might consider selling something else. But everyone you are selling against will also have enthusiasm as a given as well. Besides, I've seen salespeople so pumped up with this approach that they turn off clients because they come off like mindless zombies. Getting your client excited about your product is more about the thinking of your customer and less about the level of enthusiasm you modulate toward her. Getting your client enthusiastic about your product starts with carefully listening for the emotional clues that will tell you what gets her excited about the product you sell.

First off, consider that enthusiasm is emotional, not logical. I once was trying to sell a client into my magazine and out of a competitor's. In our first meeting the client told me he was using my competitor because that magazine had a bigger circulation and covered topics relating to his product more often. Since neither of these statements was really true, I felt that I would have an easy time making the sale. I pulled out audit statements that proved we had a larger circulation and took out tables of contents and went through them to clearly prove that we covered the topics relating to his products more often. Instead of buying from me he said, "Well I hear what you say, but it's just the feeling that their magazine is better for me." The answers to logical questions like, "Why are you buying the current product?" will rarely tell you the true emotional reasons why a client buys. Clients get enthusiastic about products for their own reasons, not yours. Real client enthusiasm is very personal. More often than not it has little to do with your product itself; it has more to do with how your product fits into the client's needs. If you are enthusiastic about the different features your product has, that's great, but clients are more often interested in how these features specifically relate to their businesses and can benefit them in very specific ways. Generating client enthusiasm means listening for these clues. Probe if necessary with questions like, "What things get you most excited about the product I sell?" "What are the best things for your company about the product I sell?" Sometimes when you really get to know a client and you find out what these appeals or "hot buttons" are, they sound ludicrous. Sometimes the craziest things come out.

5. Pick a fight.

It's not my personal style to sell this way, but there are times when I have seen this work. If you are dealing with an insecure client and think you can really prove that buying from your competition will be a tremendous mistake, then staging a confrontation can be an effective way to turn the tide. I have never been able to pull this off and think it's too risky for most people ever to attempt, but I know several salespeople who are masters of it. Here's how you do it: On a call when you hear the buy is going to a competitor, just go crazy, drop all pretense of professionalism, tell your client that you think she is making a terrible mistake, and really press her to reconsider. If she does not reconsider, make a scene, confront her, push her, and do not take no for an answer until she either backs down or asks you to leave. The strange thing is that most often people just don't throw you out of their office. Very often, insecure clients fear a confrontation that may reflect badly on them more than anything else in the world and will often reconsider buying your product if you scream for it. Sometimes this works in another way: The client thinks that if you believe in your product strongly enough to really fight hard for it, that there must be something to it. The real key to success with this approach is knowing that you have a winning hand before you make the scene and that you're dealing with a client who is not in a really secure situation. If you go in and win the sale, most often all will be forgiven, but if you do not get the order, you may have burned this bridge behind you forever.

6. Get yourself invited to make a hard competitive presentation.

Your best chance to get business away from a competitor is very often to make a hard competitive us-versus-them presentation. But client resistance to this kind of presentation is usually very high. Aside from the problem of your client "owning" the buy, there is the other problem that if you start beating up your competitor's product, you may arouse a natural reaction in your client to defend the product that has no one in the room to defend it. Your client may think, "Hey, this product isn't so bad and no one is here to defend it, so I'm going to step in and do it myself." This is disastrous: You are getting your client to defend buying a competitive product. The way around this is to get your client to "invite" you to make the competitive presentation. Psychologically this sets your client up to listen to what you have to say. She may "own" the buying of your competitor's product, but if she also "owns" the invitation to let you present a case opposing it, very often the emotional side of the buy will work much more in your favor. Here are several ways to get invited to make a competitive presentation:

a. Give the client a challenge. I once got invited to make a competitive presentation by betting a client that I could prove to him that my show product was better than the one he was now buying. He told me he doubted I could do it, and we arranged for a shoot-out where I got one hour and so did my competitor. Part of the interest in allowing a head-to-head presentation like this was for the opportunity to watch me fall flat on my face. No matter, I got my shot at the presentation and I got the order.

b. Appeal to the good of the company to hear all points of view. Say something like, "Look, you have to buy the best product, so why not look for a side-by-side comparison? It's in the best interest of your company."

c. If you can uncover a situation where a competitor made inroads on your product based on faulty information, cry foul and ask for a side-by-side shoot-out.

d. If your competition attacks you overtly, first of all say thank you. Your competitor has paid you the highest compliment (translation: "You are a force to be reckoned with and we feel you are a threat"). Then tell your client you feel the need to defend yourself from the marketplace by repudiating these slanderous comments. After you have defended your product point by point, you can then go on to make several of your own.

7. Get the overall budget increased for the purchase of your product category.

OK, your client is buying from a competitor. One way to get your product bought is to have your product, not your competitor's, listed on the buying schedule, but another way to do it is just to get the entire pie increased in size. This really depends on the kind of product you sell, but for many products it is possible to go in and do a more consultative sell and get your client to simply use more of the kind of product you are selling. If you bring a new idea of how your product can be used to increase business or save more money, more of your product may be purchased.

8. Talk about your competition.

I'm not going to give you an ethical pitch on what to say about your competition; this is not a question about ethics, but about effectiveness. You may have your own sense about what is proper or not based on your own selling experience, but selling varies tremendously from business to business. I know very successful salespeople who go for the throat on every call and take every opportunity to knock their competitors. I know other very successful salespeople who take the high road and talk about their competition only when asked about it. I believe the best approach depends on how your individual client wants to be handled. I call on some clients who by nature are very competitive people who like a good fight. They want you to fight for their business, and taking the high road may sound like a cop-out to them, or may sound as if you are just dispassionate about the product you are selling. Other clients really hate this kind of competitive talk and will tell you that you are cheapening your own hand when you speak ill of a competitive product. I believe you have to be sensitive to read these signals and the people and organizations you call on, and act accordingly. One way to read this situation is that people and companies tend to sell themselves and their own products the way they like to be sold themselves. Take some time in the waiting room to read up on the company, and see how it sells its products to its customers. Read a few trade ads; visit a trade show booth; review a sales brochure for these signals.

Closing Strategies

1. Give her a way out.

This is the biggest issue in closing when your client is buying from a competitor. It's a face-saving device, if you will, that says, "It was OK to buy a competitive product then, and it's OK to buy my product now." Here are several approaches that you can use to lead up to asking for the order.

   a. *"That was then, this is now."* Point out how things have changed, how products or markets or the company needs are different. It was OK to buy from them back then because things were different. It's OK to buy from me now because things have changed.

b. *The "whole new ball game" approach.* Take a few product enhancements that have been built into your product and make a whole big scene out of it. Make it sound as if it's simply a much bigger deal than it ever has been before. Talk about how these changes represent a whole new ball game in how these products should be evaluated. Again, you are presenting a "that was then, this is now" kind of situation.

c. *"They are not what they used to be."* Describe how your competitors simply are not as big a presence in the market and that this warrants a reevaluation. It was OK to buy from them in the past because they were much bigger, but it's OK to buy from you now because they aren't anymore.

2. Say, "Let's keep your current supplier on his toes."

Sell your client on the idea that it is to her advantage to have a second supplier, simply because it will send a message to her current supplier that he cannot take her business for granted.

3. Sell the idea of a zero-based review as the best way for the company to get the best buy for the dollar.

If you can sell all the involved decision makers on this idea, the inevitable result will be a shoot-out of competitive products, and you get your best shot.

4. Tell her that someday she will need a backup supplier.

What if the current supplier gets an order problem or runs out of material, or has a fire or gets hit by a tornado or gets hit by import tariffs? It's always to good to have a backup supplier— and why not me?

5. Say, "It's my fault."

Tell her that the reason she didn't know how terrific your product would be for her needs is because you simply screwed up.

"I don't know what got into my head, but I've never called on you before. I realize now that I should have done it years ago. Boy, did I screw up. But just because I made a mistake doesn't mean that you shouldn't reconsider your buy and consider my product as part of a mix."

6. Ask for a shoot-out.

Ask for a head-to-head, face-to-face shoot-out where you come in and present your product for an hour, and then your competitors have exactly the same amount of time to do the same.

11

The Client Who Buys Elsewhere on Relationships

From the Tough Calls survey:

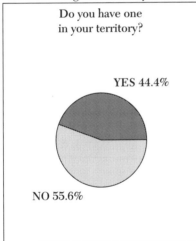

Do you have one
in your territory?

YES 44.4%

NO 55.6%

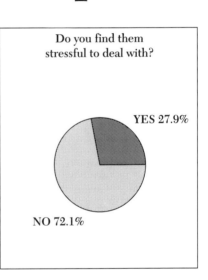

Do you find them
stressful to deal with?

YES 27.9%

NO 72.1%

This is the one place where human personality is the only criteria. It is very difficult and time-consuming to overcome."

Owner/Saleswoman, safety products company,
Fort Lauderdale, Fla.

Selling against an established relationship is tough. Relationships give your competitor an unfair advantage. He simply has access to the client's time more often than you do, and if he is smart, he will use that access to defend his turf from competitors like you.

From the outside, a well-established relationship can look invincible, but from the inside looking out, it may not look nearly as secure. You probably have accounts where you have the inside track and a competitor is locked out. Through your ongoing relationship with a client, you hear about and can respond to competitive moves as they come up. This gives you an advantage, but it is not a guaranteed lock. Whenever I am selling against an established relationship I think of two things that put this into perspective. First, I think of all the "unbreakable" relationships I have sold against in which the salesperson eventually retired. When I ask the client how the retired salesperson is, I often hear something like, "Oh, he moved to Florida and plays a lot of golf. No one much talks to him anymore." If this was such a tight relationship, why aren't they still in touch? A well-established client relationship may seem like a marriage when you start selling against it, but it isn't. It is a business relationship, based on business transactions. This is fundamentally different from more personal relationships and will always be sensitive and vulnerable to changing times and circumstances.

Second, I have seen several salespeople who had "airtight" relationships with their client base get hired away by a competitive organization with the express purpose of taking the clients with them. While hiring away the representative with the relationships gave them access to people they did not have before, moving business was quite another matter. I have seen more spectacular flops than successes with this strategy. When you work in sales or account servicing, it really does seem that everything is based on the client relationship. I have had lots of conversations with fellow salespeople where we mapped out entire sales territories account by account in terms of relationships defining where the business comes from, but if one of those clients overheard this conversation, he would think it absurd. From the client's point of view, the relationship is important, but it's not the whole show.

The good news about people who buy on relationships is that they are most often very confident buyers. If they had to justify every buying decision to others, they would be more involved in the details of the purchase. Often, if you can win over someone who buys on relationships, you can get his business pretty quickly.

Pitfalls

1. Getting competitive before you have proved yourself.

If you are up against an established relationship, sometimes getting aggressive too quickly can backfire. It is likely that any competitive argument you put forward will be reviewed by your client and the representative you are selling against. If you get very competitive while the rep you are selling against has this kind of inside track, you can get pushed out of the account forever.

That's what happened to me while I was calling on a major manufacturer of antennas. I knew that my product was far better than the one this client was buying, and I got competitive right on my first call. The client thought it all made very good sense and told me he wanted to run my presentation by a few people. I did not realize that one of these "few people" was a competitor who currently had his business and with whom he was very tight. This competing representative would have lost his client's business if the client bought my proposal. Instead of disputing my presentation, he attacked my unestablished personal credibility. Suddenly everything changed, and the client stopped taking my calls. Months later I saw him at a trade show, and as I approached the booth he moved to the other side. I approached him again several times when he was not otherwise engaged, and he moved away from me again and again. Finally I got the message and raced to get my manager, who came in and met with him. The first words out of his mouth were, "Keep Josh Gordon away from me!" My boss untangled the events and we normalized relations, but I never did get this account's business until after this client moved on to another company.

When you're selling against an established relationship, the people you sell against have the inside track. If you're an unproven commodity to the client, your arguments may not stand on their own and are much more likely to be reviewed and evaluated in the presence of the person you are directly selling against. From the inside it is easy to defend against people who are trying to get business who have no personal credibility.

2. Chasing every trivial objection.

These kinds of accounts can make you crazy. At some point the objections that get thrown at you are so trivial it makes you mad, but even if you find ways to overcome every one, more will come up. Selling this kind of account is less about answering objections and more about making your client feel comfortable doing business with you. Refocus your efforts on the relationship. Often if you build a successful relationship, the petty objections go away.

3. Getting focused on a competitive product sell.

Your client is buying a product from your competitor Joe, but the real product he is buying is not the physical product, but Joe himself. Unfortunately, you cannot really give a competitive sell against Joe since your client is friends with him. This sell is not about products, it's about relationships.

4. Giving up too early.

A well-established relationship takes months if not years to sell against. You have to look for incremental victories, dig in for a long siege, and keep on going.

Selling Strategies

1. Build your own relationship.

Selling against an established relationship takes time, says Evan Krachman of Nikon. "You can't just walk in and expect them to buy right away. They have to get to know you as a person, as a friend, as someone who has other interests, a family, etc." You might start by asking, what is my client looking for in a relationship? Different clients have different expectations as to what a buyer-seller relationship might mean. If you can look for the re-

lationship "hot button," you may succeed more quickly. Here
are several:

a. *"I buy from the organization that sends me the most credible
   representative."* This client might say, "I have to evaluate the company I am buying from. There is no way I
   can meet every single employee from these competing
   organizations, but the one thing I can do is to evaluate
   the person standing in my office." This is not such a
   crazy idea. If the salesperson calling on you is well
   trained and motivated, it is likely that the people creating the actual product you buy are similarly well trained
   and motivated. For this client you are the company. Em-
   phasizing professionalism and product knowledge can
   help get this kind of relationship started.
b. *"I buy from people I trust."* This person typically does not
   have time to really get into the details of every purchase.
   He buys from people whom he trusts will take care of
   him without hassle or requiring a lot of his attention. He
   wants you to take care of both sides of the day-to-day
   selling negotiation. You can get the relationship started
   by giving him some kind of preferential treatment or attention, giving him good pricing even though he does
   not overtly demand it, and making him think that you
   will excel at customer service and watch all the details
   of his business.
c. *"I buy from people who are my friends."* There are many
   people in business who really have no personal life
   worth talking about and like to buy from people who
   satisfy their need for friendships. They really just don't
   care which product they buy and feel that a good lunch
   or a good time now and again will tip the scale one way
   or another. This kind of relationship starts with entertaining, which your client will be only too eager to accept. Here it's better to be well liked and thought of as a
   friend than necessarily have the most persuasive case.
d. *"I buy from the representative who understands me."* There
   are a lot of service-oriented businesses where the rapport
   between the company and the representative is a very
   critical part of the product. But more than that, if a client

feels that you understand him and his needs, he will be much more eager to do business with you.

e. *"I buy from the representative who helps me look good."* If you are a true consultative salesperson and you can help your client do more than just buy your product, then the added value you bring to the table can be worth more.

2. Ask yourself whether your client is ambitious and looking for a relationship to help him get ahead.

Lonely and looking for love in all the wrong places, too busy to handle the details and looking for help, or just not really caring where he buys from as long as it's a friend—these are all different variations of the same theme. A situation where a relationship is the value added that tips the scale in your favor. If you can understand what kind of motivation your client has for getting involved in these relationships, you can get in much more quickly.

3. Envision yourself turning the account around.

Selling against established relationships takes far longer than we like to think about. Depending on the sales cycle of your product, it could take months or even years. Here is the time line of a successful turnaround that I once pulled off. The process took three years.

Phase 1: Getting on the playing field—six months. At first no one would take my calls. I was the consummate professional and did everything the books on selling tell you to do. I was nice, asked to be helpful, did not waste anyone's time, took notes on the few personal details people would share with me, and followed up by sending cute notes and articles. Our dialogue started slowly and I kept hearing about Joe, the guy I was selling against, from my client. An occasional "Joe says this," and "Joe says that" were thrown into the conversations. After about six months people began to respect me, they took my phone calls, made time to see me when I was in town, and returned my calls. A basic buyer-seller relationship was established.

Phase 2: Some personal time at last, one year. Finally, I had lunch with the client, my first personal time with him. The lunch started off a bit strained and businesslike, but by the end we were talking about our kids and outside interests. Toward the end of lunch my client said, "Hey, wait until Joe hears that we had lunch together! Boy, will he be pissed." The client was starting to get to know me more as a person.

Phase 3: Getting my foot in the door, six months. This took the form of a tiny order, a very small opportunity, but it was a start. I merchandised the heck out of it and made the client feel that he had placed a huge order with my company. I made that small order seem like the moon landing. While I was doing this my competitor was asleep at the switch. Joe was so confident that his relationship would hold his business in place that he was not keeping up with the growing dialogue I was starting with his client.

Phase 4: Starting to make inroads, six months. Finally, after they got to know me and tested my product, they were starting to take my proposal seriously. I did not get the business that year, but everyone on the account felt bad when I didn't get it and said so. My relationship was gaining ground and the rep I was selling against did not like it. He could not believe that his buddies of all these years would even consider buying from a competitor who had been locked out for so long. At one point, my clients said, "Boy, Joe is upset that we considered you for that last order, but we have to do what's right for the company."

Phase 5: Getting the business, six months. Finally, they bought. They split the business between Joe and me. I have found that established relationships are the hardest to sell against initially, but once they start to unravel they often fall apart much more quickly than other kinds of sells. If you have ever successfully undermined an established relationship sell, it is almost scary what happens. I have heard, "We must have been crazy to have given Joe all that business all those years. What were we thinking?" I have also seen a representative on the collapsing relationship sell take it personally, get offended, make a scene, and totally shoot himself in the foot for the future.

Here are some strategies you may find helpful for this final phase:

a. *Tell them it is business.* Evan Krachman of Nikon once successfully sold a new dealer on his lenses by looking him in the eye and saying, "Look, relationships aside, profit is profit. You can be best friends with representatives of those other companies, but business has got to be business." Then he made the dealer a terrific offer, asked for the order, and got it.

b. *Get your boss involved.* Sometimes it's easier for your boss to get past an established relationship. This traditional approach of going over someone's head has special application here since it is possible that there is no defending relationship protecting the account one level up, and if things are looked at objectively, the buy may be reevaluated. However, going over someone's head is not to be taken lightly. (Check Chapter 4 for details.)

c. *See whether you can educate your client on the details.* Often a client who buys on relationships does so because he does not understand the differences between the products. He may just not have the time to sit down and figure it all out and would appreciate your doing the homework for him. Often, however, clients who don't know the details don't know them for a reason. They may not care or may be working hard for a promotion where these details are unimportant.

d. *Get involved with your client's peers.* If your client buys on relationships, he probably values them and uses them in other ways besides buying things. He may spend time networking at business organizations, social scenes, and association gatherings. You can join these associations yourself or find out whom he is friendly with in these groups and spend some time with them, too. If a peer recommends to him that he should listen to you, he may listen a lot more closely.

e. *Ask for an objective shoot-out.* Relationship buys stay in place when they are left undisturbed. One way to shake them out is to ask for a highly visible head-to-head comparison of the actual products. If a comparison attracts the attention of others in the organization, it may be difficult to achieve a relationship buy continuance.

f. *Monitor the relationship you are selling against.* You have to be subtle, but you can often bring up your competitor on a call in a way that will make your client offer a comment. Every business relationship goes through ups and downs. Even the tightest relationships are tested when things go wrong. If you know when these weak times are, you can get more active. A counter-proposal always looks much better after the incumbent who has the business has just botched the job.

g. *Plan ahead to use the backlash of turnover.* Sales based on relationships are the most volatile of all. If your competitor has established a relationship with a client—and that client retires, moves on to another company, or gets promoted—the relationship leaves with him. Sometimes a new person will come in and want to know why the company bought from this person and that organization. He may want to put his own stamp on things. This is a time when every representative needs to be much more active, but when there has been a buy directed because of a relationship, the incumbent is extremely vulnerable. Products bought for logical reasons find easier transitions to new personnel. There are reports around for justification. But the relationship leaves with the people as they walk out the door. Someone might ask, "Why did we buy all this stuff from Joe all those years?" A coworker might say, "Oh, because Tom and Joe were golf buddies."

Closing Strategies

1. Ask for a level playing field.

Acknowledge the fact that your client has a relationship with a competitive representative and then ask him to look objectively at your two proposals. Ask him how would he evaluate this buy if the relationships were put aside.

2. Use the "join the club" close.

Present him with a list of all the other people who are using your product whom he might have a relationship with, then ask for the order. If a client sees his business world through relationships, this might be especially persuasive.

3. Entertain, then ask for the order.

With a client who buys on relationships, entertainment is key. There are many salespeople who may not get far enough along in the process to be allowed to entertain. For some, the fact that you are taking the client to dinner is a statement that you are halfway to making the sale. Entertainment is an unpressured time when you can get to know your client and they can get to know you.

With relationship-oriented clients, a hard sell over lunch or dinner may not be the best way to go. I've always used these occasions to seek big picture agreement at the lunch or dinner table and agree to work the details out later when we are back in the office.

It is very typical for my sales proposal to sit on a client's desk for weeks, then we have lunch. Over lunch we talk about the proposal in general terms. Toward the end of the meal we agree to go forward and work out the details. It's as though the entertainment was the social "seal of approval" that closed the sale.

12

The Client Who Buys Elsewhere Because of Company Politics

From the Tough Calls survey:

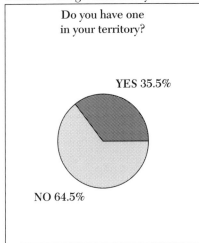

Do you have one
in your territory?

YES 35.5%

NO 64.5%

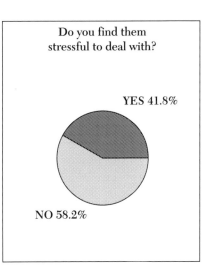

Do you find them
stressful to deal with?

YES 41.8%

NO 58.2%

*"Changing the inner political workings of another company from
the position of a supplier is nearly impossible."*

Advertising Account Executive, Hartford, Conn.

Buying is an act of power. From your point of view, a sale occurs when someone buys your product, but from a highly political organization's point of view, a sale is a defining moment where organizational power is spelled out. There are winners and there are losers. The individual or department who wins control of the purchase will likely control its implementation, control these purchases in the future, and control the budget for these purchases. Never underestimate the amount of internal posturing that may be going on to get control of the buying process. Successful selling to a very political organization means either playing to the politics of the situation or helping the person you call on to do the same. Directly or indirectly, you are not selling an individual; you are selling an organization. For salespeople the most dangerous kind of politics is what's hidden from view. You click with the person you call on and expect a big order, and when it does not come through she shrugs her shoulders and says sadly, "I wanted to buy your product, but, you know, it's politics."

Selling a political organization is more about listening than pitching. If you listen carefully and ask some probing questions, you find many subtle political signals that will help direct your selling. You are listening carefully for the shifting lines of internal conflict that will affect the buying of your product. There are natural departmental conflicts in most organizations, such as the home office versus regional offices, engineering versus marketing, international versus domestic, line management versus corporate management, and so on. Or it may be more a case of one executive versus another. The kind of political signals you are listening for will tell you who is on the way up and who is on the way out. Ultimately you are listening for who the real buying influences are and for what kind of appeal or information it will take to sell them.

One tip-off that you are dealing with a highly political buying process is when the buyer you are calling on keeps talking in terms of "we" instead of "I." When she says "we" will be reviewing your proposal, believe her.

If your client admits that her organization is "very political," she may be telling you that she is not significantly involved in the buying process. From the outside looking in, the motivation for buying may seem political, but the same behavior viewed from the inside looking out may be seen as "looking at the bigger picture for the good of the organization," "give and take between departments," or "prioritizing corporate resources." If the person you call on labels all this as political, consider that real buying decisions may be beyond her realm of understanding or control. If you suspect that the person you call on has no buying authority, refer to Chapter 4.

Pitfalls

1. Assuming that having the better product will win the sale.

In a political organization, buying decisions can resemble little courtroom dramas where different executives or departments present their cases for swaying the buying decision one way or another. When control of the buy is the number one priority, getting the best product for the best price comes second.

2. Attacking the political buying as being stupid.

Political buys are often stupid, but political buys are just as often very personal. Typically, the influence being felt when a buy goes political is from higher up in the organization. You are not going to make points by implying that organizational superiors are morons.

3. Assuming that your buyer is going to "Fight City Hall" to get your product bought.

You call on the contact and sell her on your product. She tells you she is sold and wants her organization to buy it, but to get your product bought she has to sell others in her organization. In a highly political organization without extra involvement from you, this almost never works. In a very political organization, most buyers will drop your product and run for cover at the first sign of trouble.

4. Walking away from a situation because it seems hopeless.

It can seem as if your efforts are endless and disappearing into a big black hole, but sometimes it's not that the situation is hopeless; it is just that it takes a longer time. When a political organization makes buying decisions, it involves many people who may or may not get along. This kind of extra interfacing takes extra time, but it also creates momentum. This momentum may work against you when you are first selling them, but it works for you when you have the business.

Selling Strategies

1. Clarify objections and ask who raised them.

If you are going to sell an organization through the person you call on, you need to get very specific about who said what. Do not assume that internal communication is good at the company you are calling on. I once could not get my product bought because the person I was calling on heard a negative comment about my product from his company president. This buyer rarely talked to the company president, so the comment had a huge impact on his behavior. A few months later I was at a trade show and had occasion to be introduced to the company president. Without mentioning the buyer by name I casually worked his comment into our conversation. He was shocked and told me that he had never said such a thing and was probably having a bad day. When I clarified this with my buyer, I got the sale. If clarifying the objection alone won't get the sale, by asking who raised it, you will begin to understand who it is you really have to sell. A good open-ended question to get this conversation started could be, "How do other people in your organization feel about my product?"

2. Use a company-specific benefit to change the perception of your product.

When you sell a product to a buyer, the details of your product are all-important, but a political sell is more conceptual. People who influence from afar are buying more on the perception of your product and of your company and much less on actual product details. Screaming about "the facts" is rarely effective when trying to sell people who are not involved with them.

Company-specific ideas or concepts will travel the political hallways far better than product facts. If you understand your client's business well and can translate your product's benefits into company-specific benefits, you will be able to do this.

If your product costs more but will speed up the production of ice cream bars, find out why this might benefit the specific company you call on. In sales letters and presentations, position your product into the company by saying, "By speeding up the manufacturing of ice cream bars, the ABC Ice Cream Company can ship three flavors a day instead of just two." Suddenly, the vice-president of flavor distribution becomes your biggest advocate and you get the buy instead of your cheaper competitors. Don't talk about the specs of your system's speed; talk about ice cream bars.

3. Use top-down political pressure indirectly or directly.

a. *Directly:* If you know the president of a company (or the top buying influence), you may think the sale is in the bag. But in more professionally managed companies, having a high-level contact does not guarantee a sale. I once encountered a situation where I had a working relationship with the president of a company, but I was still not getting business from the person two levels below whom I called on. When I would mention this to the president he would say, "Josh, I'm a professional manager. How is it going to look if I start telling my people what to buy based on relationships that I maintain from previous situations?" Better managers will make you earn the sale with their subordinates. But this doesn't mean that high-level contacts aren't helpful. High-level contacts get you favorable access to the decision-making process. Sometimes it takes a while, but over the long term, downward influence usually wins out. If you can sell to the point where your product ties with the current vendor, the downward pressure will often make the case for a tie-breaker in your favor.

b. *Indirectly:* Create the illusion of being politically connected. Since politics is more about perception than substance, why not create the perception of political friends in high places? At less political companies this might just produce a big "So what?" but to a buyer in a political organization, concern over how her buying decisions are being perceived by those above her can be very powerful. Here are some approaches I've seen used in the field.

Once while selling in the cable TV industry I was puzzled by the behavior of my manager. We were sitting in the audience at an industry trade show listening to a panel of the presidents and CEOs of major cable TV networks share their views. These were people several levels up from those we would call on to sell, yet my boss was taking copious notes. When I asked him what he was doing, he told me he was collecting enough detail to write an intelligent-sounding letter to each one. Those letters would find their way to the people he would call on several levels down in the organization, creating the illusion that he had contact with their superiors and thus some influence.

While selling to a major electrical component company I arranged a luncheon meeting at a major industry event. My boss and my boss's boss were there; I was the lowest-ranking person in attendance. The company's CEO came to the lunch, and so did several of his top people. As the discussion shifted into a high-level conversation about the details of the electrical component business, there was little I could do to add to the conversation, but after the lunch I sent a thank-you letter to the CEO. In the letter I mentioned in passing that I had set up the lunch, and commented on two key points he had made. I circulated the letter to everyone I had ever called on at that company. In reality I had spent very little actual time talking to their CEO, but to the people being copied in my letter, it looked as if I had invited him out to lunch and had had a nice conversation with him.

I once had a saleswoman working for me who really knew how to work a room strategically to her political advantage. At a reception sponsored by an organization she was trying to sell, I saw her do the following: First, she located her buyer and the CEO of the company. Then she stood with me, making small talk until the moment she was waiting for came up, and then she made her move. She approached the CEO and exchanged some charming pleasantries and a few jokes, and while she did this she shifted her position and that of the CEO about seven feet, right into the path of the buyer. With a quick turn of her head she acknowledged her buyer and brought him into the conversation. She then told the CEO how great a job he was doing and what a delight he was to work with. The exchange lasted no more than a few minutes, but she had created the illusion that she had a relationship with the company's CEO and was willing to use it to the buyer's favor.

c. *Indirectly:* Sell to the CEO's values. One of the main jobs a president or CEO does is to shape the corporate culture of the company. Sometimes you can play to the politics of an organization by reading the corporate culture and playing to its values. For instance, while in the waiting room of a new account I noticed that there were two award plaques given to the company for being a quality supplier. There was another plaque on the wall awarded to the company for passing its ISO 9000 quality audit. On the reception table was the company newsletter with an article reporting on how the CEO gave an award to an employee who had come up with an idea to improve the quality of the company's products. On the call I made a big hit by playing to that value of quality and took extra care to specifically show how my product was of higher quality than what the company was currently buying. When I was done, the buyer said, "This is really great. There are a lot of other people who will be very interested in what you have to say here. It made a lot of sense to me." Maybe I didn't have the CEO in the room helping me along, but by playing to the values he helped instill in his organization, he was just as helpful.

There are other ways to get at a company's CEO's values. Buy a few shares of stock in the company so that you can attend annual shareholders' meetings and receive company literature. Or just get an annual report or stock prospectus, or read the trade ads that the company runs in trade magazines.

4. Get other people in your organization involved with other people in their organization.

If there are many people involved in the buying decision, sometimes you can get your people to interface with their people and create a favorable perception throughout the company.
Ask:

"Can my technical person talk to your technical person?"
"Can my chief designer talk to your chief designer?"
"Can my integration engineer talk to your operations manager?"

5. Ask yourself, "How much political weight does the person I am calling on have?"

Unless you have higher political contacts, the person you call on is the conduit through which all your proposals, selling points, and arguments will flow. How well your ideas will be received depends on how much credibility and political clout this person has.

The big question is how well she gets along with her boss. Most political power flows downward. If your buyer has the faith and backing of her boss, your selling points will be taken seriously and given backing to go elsewhere in the organization. Here are some ways to get a handle on this. Ask what she thinks her boss's reaction would be to what you just presented. Make a comment about your own boss and then wait for one about hers. Tell her she does so much at her company that she should ask her boss for a raise, and wait for a reaction. If she says something like, "Well actually, my boss and I get along very well," you are probably dealing with a player. If she says, "If this goes through, maybe it will get my boss off my back for a while," you probably are not. In addition, ask, "How long have you been with the company?" and ask yourself, "Does she know her stuff?"

6. Ask yourself how you can make your buyer look like a hero.

When selling a political organization it is very helpful to have an advocate for your product whom you can work with. The shifting tide of political power can move too quickly for you to really react unless you have an inside person looking out for you. If you can help your contact look like a hero, you will win an advocate and also strengthen the hand of that advocate in the political arena where she fights for you.

7. Get your buyer angry about politics.

Buyers who have to deal with a lot of meddling politicians are often unhappy campers; they are put out in the front lines and asked to defend decisions they have little input in making. If you can get them to complain about the political mess they are in the middle of, they will often share with you details that will help you sell the people they have to work with.

8. Ask for a group meeting.

Buying decisions made in a group meeting with everyone involved in a buying process tend to stick. If someone changes her mind, it's just too much trouble to get all those people to sit down together again. Occasionally it is easy to get a group meeting; sometimes just asking as an outside party with a different point of view will get a gathering together. However, I find this is rare. More often clients are too busy and do not want to make the kind of time commitment it takes to hold a group meeting. Before you ask for a group meeting, ask yourself why one has not already happened without your prompting. You are advocating a purchase that all these people are involved with, so why have they not met together before? Unless you are selling a unique product, it is very hard to get all the decision makers to sit down with you at one time. Often the higher-level people are ones who would not sit down with you individually, so why would they go the extra step and meet as a group? What you need is something different or new to generate excitement for a group meeting: information from a new research report, a new idea that will help their business, or the introduction of a new service or feature.

You can also try an informal approach. If you can get a corporate superior to sit down to a lunch, you can often get conflicting parties who report to her to do the same. Groups that meet socially together will often find ways to work out their differences.

9. Send a promotion to everyone in the company.

If you can come up with a truly compelling rationale for buying and some significant documentation proving it, put it in a promotional piece and send it to everyone in the organization. This works especially well in a political organization because when people start forwarding your memo to one another, it implies acceptance of the ideas. I once sent a promotional letter to everyone at a company that I was trying to sell. The company president received a copy and, since he was not directly involved in this part of the business, forwarded it routinely to the person who was. This was the very person whom I usually dealt with. He was so impressed that the president had sent him my memo that he took it very seriously!

Closing Strategies

1. Convey the hidden message: "It will help your career to buy from us."

The person who is buying sees buying as a way to move up the corporate ladder first and buying the best products at the best price second. Tell her how smart buyers who want to be perceived as up-and-coming stars are buying from you, then ask for the order.

2. Show how buying your product poses no risk.

Buyers in political organizations spend a lot of time covering their butts. Somehow you have to structure your sale so that it presents minimal or no risk. If you are the market leader, play this up. If you aren't, offer a guarantee to make your buy risk-free, then ask for the order.

3. Ask for the order in front of everyone.

If you can get a group meeting, ask for the order before anyone leaves the room. Commitments made in front of a group have a habit of sticking.

4. Use a written selling proposal.

Again, a lot of people are involved in the buying process in a political organization, many of whom you will never meet. Close your order with a written proposal, and put enough selling information in the proposal so that anyone picking it up has all the information needed to make an intelligent buying decision.

13

The Client Who
Is Indifferent

From the Tough Calls survey:

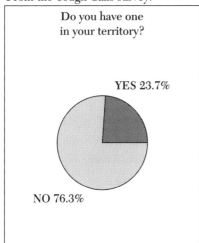

Do you have one
in your territory?

YES 23.7%

NO 76.3%

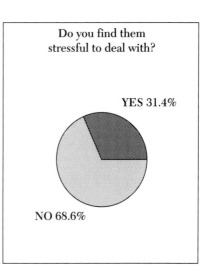

Do you find them
stressful to deal with?

YES 31.4%

NO 68.6%

*"Real decision makers are increasingly 'hidden' from day-to-day
business transactions. 'Replacements' for buyers have little experience, no desire to learn, and are powerless to make decisions.
When it comes to my product, few get excited."*

Advertising Salesman, Providence, R.I.

You are all pumped up for giving the big presentation you have
worked on for days, but when you look up at your client's face,
you see boredom written all over it. You quicken the pace and
punch your lines harder. Your client yawns, looks at her watch,
and casually reminds you that she has another meeting in five

minutes. You spent so much time getting ready for this call; you were so enthusiastic. Why wasn't she?

Most of the talk about enthusiasm in sales is misplaced. Although it is critical to represent your product and your company with enthusiasm, for a sales representative enthusiasm is a given. The real issue is not about the level of enthusiasm you project at your client, it is about how much enthusiasm you can generate within your client for yourself and the product you sell. The key is to get inside your client's head and present your product so that your client sees it as something she can get excited about. You need to be intuitive, flexible, and responsive to your client's state of mind.

Pitfalls

1. Trying to control the call too much.

The path to a sale is slightly different for every client. For some clients the path is clear and straight; for others there will be twists, turns and surprises; but one thing that always points the way to the sale is when your client is interested in what you are saying. If your client loses interest, you have strayed from the path. I have seen a lot of salespeople get mistrained early on to control presentations completely. They are told that a successful presentation is one in which you start at the beginning, exercise complete control, make every point included in your presentation while overcoming objections along the way, and ask for the order at the end. Sometimes this approach misses the dialogue that would actually lead to a sale. Clients buy for their reasons, not yours. Without a two-way dialogue you are flying blind.

2. Thinking the call is going badly because "she just doesn't want to listen to what I have to say."

In sales, communication is your responsibility. If your client is not listening to you it is not her fault. If you perceive that your client is not listening while you are giving a presentation, you have to immediately rethink your call. If it means throwing out the presentation you spent hours preparing, out it goes.

3. *Not customizing the call for your client.*

The biggest cause of indifference and boredom among clients is when a salesperson shows up and gives a canned presentation with no sensitivity to the client. Your basic product presentation is a valuable tool to begin with, but it needs to be adapted to the unique needs of every client.

Selling Strategies

1. *Prepare for a unique call.*

If your client is indifferent to you on your first call, don't be surprised. Most clients find sales presentations boring. If you actually show up on a call with a presentation that is really interesting, you will stand out. The best way to fight indifference on a call is before the call.

Here are some ideas on how to achieve this:

a. *Call ahead.* A day or two before your sales visit, call your client and ask her whether there is anything in particular that she would like you to come prepared to talk about. I find that about half the time there is, and I am able to shape my call around what my client wants to hear about. When my client declines to give me any direction, that's OK too because she appreciates the fact that I cared enough about her time and uniqueness to ask.

b. *Ask yourself, "Has this client heard it all before?"* In many territories most clients have heard the basic pitch for your product. If you know this to be the case, you had better come up with something different to talk about.

c. *Ask yourself, "Whose business is this presentation about?"* A client buys your product because it will be good for her business, not yours. You need a healthy mix of information about your product and her business. Sometimes salespeople talk only about their products. Unless a client is really ready and interested to hear about this, it can result in client indifference.

d. *Present yourself as someone who is responsive as you start your call.* Start by asking questions. Tell your client that you do not want to waste her time with information she already knows and that you want to start your call on a level that will be most useful to her. The questions you ask will be unique for your selling situation. Some basic questions to adapt to your needs could be: How familiar are you with my product? Have you ever used this kind of product before? What is it about this kind of product that makes it most valuable for you? What are you trying to accomplish by buying this kind of product?

2. Present your product in terms of her business.

Clients rarely get excited about the products that people come to show them just as products. Clients do get genuinely excited about what a product will do for them or their company. What bores most clients to death is unimportant details about your product that do not affect their business. The old story about the salesperson who bored his clients to death by talking about the details about the drill bits that he sold rings true here. He would go on calls and talk about how his drill bits were made of the finest steel and milled to the finest specifications, but what his customers were interested in all along was not his drill bits, but ¼-inch holes in pieces of wood.

3. Adjust your presenting style.

If you are on a call and you notice that your client is starting to slip away, sometimes a minor in-flight adjustment is all it takes to get your client's head back into the dialogue. Consider that different clients need different presenting styles. Some clients are emotional sells, who buy largely from their friends, while others want to be sold on pure logic. As salespeople our job is not to pass judgment on this, but rather to be flexible enough to adapt. I was once giving a flip-chart presentation and could see my client looked bored every time I pointed to some numbers, but when I started just talking he looked right at me and paid attention. Finally I said, "Would you rather I just talk you through the rest of this?" When he nodded yes, I folded up the presentation and handled the rest of it as a conversation. Some clients just want you to talk to them, while others really do want you to prove your points with numbers, technical specs, or measurable proof. In addition, there are several other continuums to consider as you adjust your presenting style:

- *Very enthusiastic . . . low-key.* Some clients genuinely appreciate an extremely upbeat positive attitude, which they will take as a sign of confidence in yourself and your product. I have also called on clients who are very low-key and withdraw when they are confronted with a big enthusiastic presentation. For them I find that toning down my approach works best to draw them out. Telemarketers are trained to mimic the talking style of the people they are trying to sell over the telephone. It's really no different in person. Your presenting style should adapt to the person you are presenting to.
- *Fast-paced . . . slower-paced.* Here again the speed of your delivery is determined by the interest your client is showing you as you are speaking.
- *More personal . . . more businesslike.* Again, this is a matter of personal style. Some clients are very formal when you first meet and warm up as time goes on.

4. Ask, "Is there something else you would like to hear about?"

Some salespeople hate this because it gives up too much control of the call to your client. I disagree: Nothing is more deadly than boring your client. You simply have to redirect your call, and this is a very direct way to invite your client to help steer things to a direction that will be more productive for her. Very often this kind of question does not result in any redirection at all, but what it does is very gently send the message to your client that you notice she is not paying attention. Very often this serves as a "raised eyebrow" that nudges your client's attention back into your presentation.

5. Ask, "Is there a better time to discuss all this when I can come back?"

As tough as it is to get in to see people, sometimes it's counterproductive to present when the client is distracted. If you sense that this is the case, asking this question can restructure things in a more productive way. I once made a call on a client whose father had just died two hours before I arrived. When I heard the news I asked whether I could come back another time. He declined, saying that he would be out making funeral arrangements for the next week and that when he got back, rescheduling would be impossible because of all the work that would have piled up. He told me that my call was going to be now or never and that he was "feeling OK." He was not OK, and in hindsight I wish I had insisted on not going forward. The problem with giving a presentation to a client who is clearly distracted is twofold: First of all, your presentation is not being taken seriously, but what's worse is that you will have given your best shot to make a sale on this account without getting any response. Say you write this call off as a lost cause. But what do you say the next time you call on this client? You can't really go over the same information all over again. More often, asking the question about whether there is a better time you can come back serves as another "raised eyebrow" that draws attention to the fact that you have noticed your client is not paying attention.

6. Call attention directly to her behavior.

If the two previous "raised eyebrow" questions did not nudge your client back into your presentation, it is time to escalate to the next step. There are several ways to do this depending on what your personal style and relationship with the client is like. Seriously: "Anne, I spent a lot of time working on this presentation, but it doesn't look as if I am really on target for you. Is this true?" With humor: "Hey, Anne, am I boring you?" With apology: "I am sorry, I thought this was the kind of presentation you would find interesting . . . (wait for a response)."

7. Ask a question you know the answer to.

If your call is going badly and your client will not help you refocus even after you have invited her to do so with the previous approaches, you need to rethink things through on your own. I find it hard to rethink and pay attention to what my client is saying at the same time. By asking a question you already know the answer to, what you are doing is buying yourself a minute or two of thinking time. While you nod politely to the answer that you already know, you have time to refocus your brain to rethink your entire presentation, then try the new approach.

8. *Ask yourself, "Am I selling what my client wants to buy?"*

What does your client want to buy? If you say, "my product, of course," you are only partly right. Beyond the physical attributes of your product is a whole intangible package of perceptions, expectations, and beliefs that affect any sale. Aside from the physical product, your client may also be buying the safety of buying from a stable company, the friendship of a salesperson, job security, the opportunity to demonstrate negotiation ability to a superior, the opportunity to make a change in suppliers that demonstrates power or control, an affiliation with the "hot new product" or "hot new company," better delivery times, better financial arrangements, extra personal attention, political security, prestige, a better price, or an affiliation with knowledgeable people who will help her company use the product she buys more effectively. Ask yourself, aside from the physical product your client buys when she buys from you, what kinds of intangible or emotional aspects of the product does she also want to buy? Excitement is emotional, and it is often the more intangible aspects of a product that build the emotional case for the sale.

9. *Ask yourself, "Is this the right person?"*

Sometimes there is no interest in your presentation because the person assigned to meet with you has no interest in your product. The person is just an information gatherer sent there to protect the valuable time of the real decision maker. If you are calling on a buffer, indifference to your presentation is natural for a person in this situation. I try to get the person to acknowledge that she is just an information gatherer and that I am there to help her gather the right information. I ask, "What kind of information is your boss really interested in hearing about?" (Also, check Chapter 4.) There is a variation on this formula: I have noticed that people who are about to be promoted or to take a job with another company also appear very indifferent on a sales call. It's very hard to really get to the bottom of this kind of indifference. Suffice it to say that if a person gets a big promotion and will no longer be involved in the kinds of products you are selling, then it's going to be very hard to get him excited. Again, the key is to see whether he can share with you the fact that he is moving on and to become an information provider for the next person through the door.

10. Ask yourself, "Is this just the way she is?"

Some clients are just low-key or intentionally buy with poker faces. It's just who they are. What drives me crazy is the low-key client who tells me a week after the fact how much she enjoyed my presentation, when during the visit I thought she was bored to death.

Closing Strategies

Getting your client's attention back from a failing presentation is a start. The next step is sustaining her interest long enough so that she makes it through the selling process and you can close her.

1. Develop a more personal relationship.

I once called on a client who was obviously bored with the buying process. I was able to keep the sale alive by developing a secondary relationship based on *Star Trek* trivia. I would call her up and talk to her about that week's show, and afterward we would talk about business proposals.

2. Just keep showing up.

I once had an account where there was a lot of interest in buying a large program during my visit. During my meeting with these people, things went great: One person was going to look into one thing and someone else into another. After I left I expected a beehive of activity that would result in a sale. This did not happen. As soon as I walked out the door, all activity regarding this purchase died immediately. I found that I just had to keep showing up to keep the excitement going. There was obviously little internal enthusiasm for the project, but I just kept showing up, and eventually the sale came through.

14

The Client Who
Is Abrasive

From the Tough Calls survey:

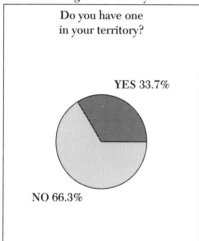

Do you have one
in your territory?

YES 33.7%

NO 66.3%

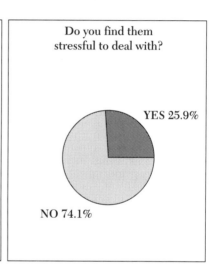

Do you find them
stressful to deal with?

YES 25.9%

NO 74.1%

"Don't take it personally, clients like this probably treat all sales-people the same."

Advertising Salesman, Chicago, Ill.

Among coworkers, abrasiveness is considered problematic and unproductive behavior. But some organizations intentionally hire abrasive people to meet with the salespeople who call on them. Their management might say, "We have to get tough on our suppliers; let's see if we can find a real SOB who will squeeze a little extra out of them." In addition, sometimes abrasive people are put in situations of buying because no one in their organization wants to deal with them face to face for long periods of time. If you are dealing with an abrasive client, chances are good that the organization who placed the person in that position knows full well what it is doing.

Strictly from a selling point of view, I view abrasiveness as a buying technique, not a personality flaw. When you first meet an abrasive client he may be very charming and personable, but make no mistake, he is summing you up. On a dime his personality will turn unpleasant and he will put you on the defensive. I never feel bad for these people with the misshapen personalities; I view their behavior as highly intentional. They want you to feel uncomfortable.

The worst abrasive clients have developed their craft over the years and know just how to zoom into you and get you defensive and crazy. Abrasive behavior is like a product from a little cottage industry with no standards and no two alike. One abrasive client I call on criticizes everything; another threatens to pull all his business on every call. Another uses a constant stream of sarcasm; another I call on explodes one day and the next day, like clockwork, apologizes and says, "Look, I know I'm being difficult, but I'm a guy who knows what he wants." Another uses "brutal honesty" to let me know where I stand, which is not very high in his estimation. In some ways selling an abrasive client may be easier than having one as a coworker, since typically the buyer-seller relationship does not include enough hours in a week for the full range of problems that abrasiveness causes. But selling someone who is abrasive is different from merely coping with him and presents different challenges.

Pitfalls

1. Not returning to the selling dialogue.

Abrasive clients have a way of setting the agenda by the pure force of their personality. They push and push until you are dancing to their tune, but if all you are doing is granting concessions and not doing any selling, then you are playing their game, not yours. You have to be relentless when you call on these people. After they hit you with yet another shot, you must defuse it and return again to the selling dialogue.

2. Falling for the "you and me against your management" game.

Several times when I've dealt with abrasive clients, they have tried to befriend me as an ally against the company I was representing. "Hey, Josh, if we could just get the same concessions out of your company as we get from everyone else in the business, I know we can do a lot of business together. I know you want to make the sale, but those people in your home office are out of touch with reality. What do you say we get together and straighten them out?" In the short term it may be flattering to be taken into such a client's confidence, but if you agree that your company's management really is out of touch with reality, it reflects badly on the product you represent.

3. Assuming that he is the only jerk at the company you call on.

I always assume that the organization I am calling on knows that this person is abrasive. When I managed a sales staff I approached the boss of a particularly abrasive client to ask whether he realized the abusive treatment representatives who called on her were receiving. His reply was, "She gets great pricing, and as long as she keeps doing that she'll be doing all the buying for us." Very often the person who is aggressively pushing you for concessions is being pushed himself.

Selling Strategies

1. Maintain the theater of the big squeeze.

What most abrasive clients want more than concessions is the illusion that they are pushing you to the wall for the benefit of their companies, especially in ways that get the notice of their bosses. This is their way of looking good in front of their management. Very often if you can create the illusion of being pressed to the wall without generating major concessions, you can do yourself and your client a lot of good. It's not about negotiations or concessions; sometimes it's about theater. Your job is to develop a starring role for your client as the guy who does miracles for his company. Once an abrasive client of mine kept pushing for major concessions and threatened to pull all his business and give it to a direct competitor. My company was organizing a high-profile industry committee meeting that would help direct the business we were selling into. We invited the client and his boss to speak at one of the sessions. It made the client look great in front of his boss and cost us two extra lunches at the session we were already running. The abrasiveness and threats stopped, at least for a few months.

Besides writing a starring role for your client, you can write one for yourself. I had to learn this the hard way when dealing with one abrasive client who kept pushing me and pushing me for concession after concession. Our negotiations dragged on and into a long sales trip I was making. Because of timing problems, I was forced to handle some details on a cellular phone call in the middle of a busy city beltway during rush hour. Suddenly he wanted an entirely different concession. I lost my temper and yelled, "Look, you have pushed me to the wall! I've come up with everything you've asked for, I'm sitting here stuck in traffic talking to you on a cellular phone, and you throw this in my face? You're driving me nuts." Suddenly he became the cool one and asked me to calm down, and then he placed the long-awaited order. When it was time to sell him again I learned my lesson. I became more emotional and theatrical. I would moan and groan about how tough he was on me. I did the moaning, he did the buying, and he became a good customer.

2. Cajole.

Humor is a terrific way to deal with abrasiveness. By making light of the abrasive behavior, the demands being made, or the intimidating behavior, you can sometimes defuse the pressure. Cajoling is also a good way to test out just how serious the demand is. If you make a joke about a demand and then change the subject, and the demand goes away, you have just gotten past it and probably avoided spending a lot of time on an objection that was not key to making the sale. If the joke falls flat and the client draws your attention to it, take a different approach. Every salesperson's style is different here. I have the best success with clients I know well when it comes to cajoling, but I know other salespeople who can cajole in the first few minutes of their first call.

3. Distinguish between behavior designed to put you on the defensive and real objections.

Don't buy the assumption that the pressure techniques that are being used on you at the moment are directly connected to the sale. Some abrasive clients sit and think what they can throw at you and make you crazy. Very often these are not real objections that need to be dealt with or overcome. More often they are unrelated to the sale and serve only as pressure points to push you onto the defensive. Sometimes it's hard to make this distinction with an abrasive client whom you do not know well. It's a question of developing a relationship with a client and an understanding of how he relates to you. One abrasive client once told me, "I think your company is going out of business, your product looks weaker than it did a year ago, and your competitors are getting very aggressive. I can buy the same product I buy from you from them for about half the price. Your management at your home office is out of touch with reality." I happened to know that this client hated my boss and that he was just blowing off steam. But with a different client this might be the beginning of a selling dialogue with a price objection as a starting point. As I mentioned above, humor is a good way to separate the real objections from the pressure tactics, but another is just to minimize the importance of it and move on. If the client brings it up again, you know that this is an important subject for him. For more information about separating the real objections from the pressure tactics, see Chapter 6.

4. Use timing to get your selling points in.

Many abrasive clients I deal with seem to throw their abrasive behavior at me in waves. I don't know what triggers their behavior, but it really does seem to turn on and off at will. At certain times they get me in their sights and just keep shooting, but I have also noticed that there are times when they behave like perfectly normal, sensible people. When they are in the normal mode I try to get as many selling points in as quickly as I can.

5. Get to the bottom line quicker.

Ask yourself, "What does he want to get by acting this way?" Very often abrasive clients do not know how to articulate their needs but are good at pushing and threatening suppliers until they come up with something that seems acceptable to them. I have called on several abrasive clients who, once we got past all the threats and belligerence, really were not asking for anything out of the ordinary; they just started off our calls with a big fuss in case they didn't get what they wanted later on in the call. When one abrasive client began pushing me, I said, "What is it you are really looking for in a product like the one I am selling?" From there I started a dialogue that led to the real issue this client needed to have addressed. Sometimes when you get off the defensive and start probing into the mind of your client for what's really important to him, strange things come up. Often the real key to selling him has nothing to do with business-related concessions. Assuming that you have competitive pricing and features, what he really may be pushing for is simply some kind of special treatment that is especially meaningful for him. With many abrasive clients, when you can read the hidden code and find what they are really looking for on a personal level, the abrasiveness disappears. One of my clients was a total horror until I discovered that she liked being taken out to lunch a lot. Once I started doing this she was like a different person. I called on one client who desperately wanted me and several members of my company to show up at his company's Christmas party every year. When we finally started doing this we began a much better relationship. The crazy thing about it is that neither of these two clients could just come out and tell me what they really wanted. Somehow through trial and error and intuition I had to decipher the hidden code.

6. Defuse pressure.

Abrasive clients are masters of pressure. In order to return to the selling dialogue you need a battery of pressure-defusing techniques:

a. *Get him into problem solving.* Ask, "If everything went your way, how would this purchase go?" Or "How would you like to see this proposal resolved?" Or "What do we have to do to make this sale happen?"

b. *If he starts to repeat himself, paraphrase back what he has just said.* When he hears his own words coming back at him, he will understand that you got his message.

c. *Interrupt the attack with a question.* Say, "I understand what you are saying; that's very interesting about x, y, z. Now let me ask you a question that relates to that. . . ." The question you ask changes the subject, and when the subject is changed, you are in control of the selling dialogue once again.

d. *Humanize your relationship.* If you can socialize with your client and get to know him on a more personal basis, it is less likely that you will be subjected to browbeating. It's really hard to pressure someone with whom you have just been out to dinner and whose company you enjoy. I have found, however, that sometimes this can backfire. In one situation a client got even more demanding after we had been out socially. "Josh, I thought we were friends. We all went out to dinner with the wives, and everyone got along beautifully. I can't believe you can't get me this one little favor from your company; what kind of moron do you work for anyway?"

e. *Have your boss be the "bad guy."* If there is a point of disagreement you cannot get past, tell him you are powerless to change anything because your boss just won't budge. Tell him he is welcome to call your boss himself or send him a letter. I have never had a client sit down and write a letter when it comes time to do this. This is really a polite way of saying no without having to say it yourself.

f. *If he says something particularly nasty, ask him if he really meant what he said.* Repeat it back to him and then ask him, "Joe, I can't believe you really meant what you said. If I understand you correctly, what you're saying is. . . ." Very often he may tell you you're being too sensitive, but the message that he overstepped his boundaries will be communicated to him.

g. *Stall.* If you are being pushed into a corner, claim you are powerless to grant the concession he is looking for and that you must consult your boss. Somehow, when you get back to him the next day, the pressure seems a lot less critical.

7. Evaluate the threats.

One of the basic tools of the abrasive client is to threaten. There are only so many threats in the buyer-seller relationship. Here are the basics:

a. You will never get my business.
b. You will lose all my business.
c. I will give your business to a competitor.
d. I will tell your boss you are incompetent.
e. I will think that you are a jerk, and will say so.
f. I will tell other clients of yours that your company is mixed up.

If you know you are going into a situation with a client who likes to threaten a lot like this, you may want to talk to your boss about a worst-case scenario before you go in. Keep in mind, too, that most abrasive clients are bluffing most of the time. Take a step back from the selling process and ask yourself just how seriously to take these threats. I have been in several situations where top management already decided to buy my product. The person doing the order placement, who had no control whatsoever over the buying process, made a big play to try to squeeze some extra blood out of me just to make himself look good. There were threats and unpleasant comments. Ultimately we ignored them and the sale went through without a hitch. It is hard to know just when to say no like this. You have to know the account well, but in a situation like this, it is not to your advantage to cave in. If you cave in to the demands of a buying agent who has no buying power, you have just given that powerless agent a lot of control over the next purchase you make. You have just created your own worst nightmare.

8. Draw a line.

Many abrasive clients need to have a boundary drawn for them that they are not allowed to cross. Unfortunately, you are often the only other person in the room who can set those boundaries. Say, "Look, I know that you want better delivery times, but this is the best we can do. We've been over this many times, and it's simply not going to change." Be firm and matter-of-fact, don't dwell on it, and move on to the next subject. If you think you might lose the business because of it, you can soften your presentation by mentioning that the concession may change at some time in the future. I have one abrasive client who will demand and demand until I say no, and then he buys. He does not seem to care what he gets; he does not even listen to what he is asking for. He is guided by one basic truth: When I am willing to walk away from his business, then he can assume that he has pushed me as far as he can and has gotten the best possible deal he can get. With some abrasive clients, telling them no will actually get you to the sale more quickly.

9. Tell him you are embarrassed.

If cajoling is not your style, I have seen more serious-minded salespeople admit to feeling uncomfortable when dealing with abrasive clients. Say, "John, I'm not used to being asked these things, so you will forgive me if it takes me some time to react," or "Nancy, these are difficult questions you are asking. I don't often feel comfortable dealing with clients in the way that you are asking me to go, but I'll do my best." Sometimes sharing your feelings about being uncomfortable is disarming to these kinds of clients and they'll lighten up on you; sometimes not.

10. Work your territory so that he is less important to you.

Life is short, and abrasive clients are often bad time management investments for your territory. Consider that if they are always threatening to cancel their business, they are not very good long-term prospects for building a territory. Also consider that the more business you get from them, the more intimidating their threats to pull their business will become. I always limit the time I spend developing business of abrasive clients and try to build up other accounts in my territory. When the abrasive client is less important to you and your territory, you will be able to deal with him with a much stronger hand.

11. Ask yourself whether you are dealing with a telephone bully.

The essence of abrasive clients' behavior is confrontation. Their constant pushing is really a controlled confrontation designed to get you crazy. It is much easier to initiate a confrontation over the phone. About half of all the abrasive clients I have called on are telephone confronters. They blast you on the phone but are perfectly delightful in person. Sell them in person; service them on the phone.

12. Consider downward pressure.

Most client bullies are being bullied themselves. If you can develop any kind of rapport with your client's boss, often the bullying stops. If you can't comfortably talk to your client's boss, possibly your boss can. Sometimes by selling the abrasive client's boss, you make it safe for him not to have to bully you.

Closing Strategies

1. Fight your way to the finish.

Get emotional. If you don't raise your voice or seem stressed, the abrasive client will not believe he's gotten the best he can out of you.

2. Sell him on the idea that he's gotten the best deal.

Explain point by point why he has squeezed real blood out of you and that he is getting a better deal than just about anybody else, then ask for the order.

3. In the closing process give a concession specially targeted to appease his boss.

In most cases, abrasive behavior is theater designed for the abrasive client's boss. If you give a concession directed at that client's boss, very often the abrasive behavior goes away—until next time.

15

The Client Who
Is Hard to Read

From the Tough Calls survey:

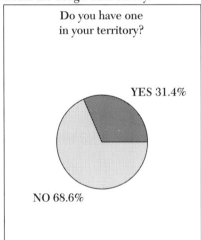

Do you have one
in your territory?

YES 31.4%

NO 68.6%

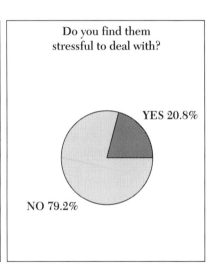

Do you find them
stressful to deal with?

YES 20.8%

NO 79.2%

"Listen carefully and learn. The less said the better when dealing with difficult clients."

Marketing Manager, marketing/communications services,
White Plains, N.Y.

You got the appointment, or did you? She is physically there in front of you, but since she doesn't react to anything you say, you wonder whether she is really there. In one extreme case I came close to poking my client's arm just to see whether he was still breathing. Another client would answer all my questions as if he were just learning how to speak English and knew only three words: yes, no, and maybe. This kind of client gives you no feedback, so you don't know what she is thinking, and she keeps her facial expressions and emotions so tightly controlled that you don't know what she is feeling. Maybe you are having a terrific call, but you would never know it, since she doesn't react to your presentations and is noncommittal about any point you make. When you leave her office you have no idea whether you have sold her or not, but a call without feedback is like no call at all. You might as well have stayed in the car.

Pitfalls

1. Trying to get the client involved by talking more.

If your client gets a little distracted on a call, you might pick up your pace, become more animated, talk more, or talk more loudly. But if your client is holding back for a specific reason, upping the noise level at your end can have the opposite effect. It can turn her off even more. Stop, look, and especially listen before you move on.

2. Assuming that you've sold her because there has been no negative feedback.

No feedback means no negative feedback, and for this you might initially be grateful. But a client who is not raising objections is a client who does not have her head in the selling dialogue. Without negative feedback or objections, you are flying blind. For more ideas on this, see Chapter 13.

3. Feeling uncomfortable.

There are many reasons why a client will clam up on you. Although it is your problem to deal with, it is not your personal problem. It may make you feel uncomfortable, but just remember that you are not doing anything wrong. Most often clamming up is a buying strategy, and it's just part of the buyer-seller relationship, so do not take it personally.

Selling Strategies

1. Ask an open-ended question and just stop talking.

If you have a client who just clams up, sometimes clamming up yourself helps get her to talk. Many clients feel uncomfortable with silence in a social situation. Silence may be golden, but it can also be used as a crowbar to pry open a client whose mouth is shut. Try to talk as little as possible and then get her to talk as much as possible. Then ask an open-ended question where there's plenty of conversational matter to discuss as a response and simply stop talking. With any luck, what comes next is the feedback you so desperately need.

2. Give her total control of the call.

Very often clients who don't give you any feedback are people who like to be in total control. I have found that many well-intentioned clients, wary of sales techniques that have gotten the best of them in the past, just clam up. But without any feedback it's going to be very difficult to sell them anything. By holding their cards so close to their vest, they do maintain total control of the call. If it is total control she wants, give it to her. It is possible that she has a very tightly orchestrated agenda in her mind that you would have to follow anyway in order to make the sale. Give control of the call by pausing a beat, then saying, "I sense that this is not so interesting for you. Is there something you would rather hear about?" Or just ask, "What shall we talk about next?"

3. Get her to talk about anything.

If you can't get the mule to go down the trail, see whether you can find a different trail. If your client does not seem to want to talk about her business needs and preferences, there is probably a reason. But to keep pushing her to open up is not going to work. Instead of pushing her again, try to get her to talk about nonbusiness subjects. It may be that a client who is not sharing feedback with you is just not comfortable with you personally yet. Sometimes talking about personal things has a way of loosening up a client's tongue so that eventually she will talk about other things that might lead to a sale.

4. Start your call by asking questions.

One way to cut off the chance that your client is going to clam up is to start the call by having your client do most of the talking. If she is reluctant, sometimes you have to sell her on the idea of starting the call with a question-and-answer session. Tell her, "I don't want to waste your time, so I would like to start the call at a level that would be most valuable for you. Can I ask a few questions to help do this?" The first question you ask might be, "How much do you know about my product?"

5. Do a trial close.

It may seem early in the call to be asking for the order, but if you have not gotten any feedback, use it to your advantage. Say, "Maybe it's a little early in our conversation, but since you have not raised any objections or concerns, I have to ask you, are you ready to place an order now?" I have found some unresponsive clients were really just laying low like cats waiting for me to ask for the order. Suddenly they came to life and I got a ton of feedback that told me they had been paying careful attention to everything I said. For other clients, asking for the order can be a wake-up call that gets their attention and helps them focus back on the call.

6. Make the call more interesting for the client.

Very often the reason a client is clamming up is that she is not interested in what you have to say. When you talk to a lot of people who do a lot of buying, they all seem to agree on one thing: that most presentations they see are boring. The best way to make a call interesting is to prepare. (More on this later in this chapter when I talk about preparing to ask questions so that your client is motivated to answer them.)

7. Do something personal to get a reaction.

How much feedback your client gives you on a call is a personal decision made by her. She can give you a lot or a little, but it is her own personal style and way of dealing with the buyer-seller relationship that determines it. You could view feedback as a personal gift from your client to you, and then reciprocate in kind by giving her a small gift of personal attention in some way. Besides personal entertaining, which often goes flat when you are trying to break a new account where you don't have a relationship, try some of these. When I worked for a research company I broke down some personal barriers by sharing some nonconfidential research on different boating manufacturers with a client who is a boating enthusiast. When I was in Europe I picked up a European dog magazine for a client who was a dog enthusiast. For a client of mine who has a shot glass collection, I sent a shot glass from Disney World. A parachuting client of mine got a magazine article naming parachuting the most dangerous sport on the planet. Compliment him on his new suit. Buy a joke card that describes her situation. Tell a funny joke. Do something unexpected.

8. Level with her.

Sometimes honesty is the best policy. If her lack of feedback is frustrating you, say, "I was surprised you haven't raised any concerns or given me any feedback, and I was starting to get concerned that what I was saying was not interesting to you. Is this true?" Encourage objections. Make it easy for her to share negative feedback with you.

9. Ask yourself why she is intentionally stonewalling you.

Sometimes you have to play detective to find out why it is actually happening. Here are some of the many situations I have encountered. Sometimes if you know what the problem is, you can handle it better.

  a. *Your client is a poker-faced negotiator.* It may be just the way she is playing it. She knows exactly what she wants and thinks that the fewer clues she gives you, the better off she will be later on when the dialogue shifts to negotiating terms and prices.
  b. *Your client is waiting for you to prove yourself.* Some clients whom you are meeting for the first time will want you

to prove yourself before they invest their time in a relationship that may or may not have payback.

c. *Your client is in a time crunch.* Offering no feedback on a call may be a way to terminate dialogue and make the call shorter.

d. *Your client has made up her mind before you got there that she is not going to buy from you.* Things may have changed since you made the appointment. If she knows she is not going to buy from you, the call is going to be a waste of her time. From her point of view, the quicker it's over the better.

e. *Your client thinks you're coming off like a jerk.* If your client wants to get rid of you more quickly, she will clam up.

f. *Your client has a very serious personality.* Some clients are just wired up this way, so don't take it personally. It's not going to change; this is just the way they are. They not only give very little feedback in their professional life, this is the way they are in their personal life as well.

g. *Your client is not a decision maker.* Sometimes a real decision maker is too busy to meet with you and sends a lower-level person to run interference. This person may not be involved in any way in the buying process, and thus has no interest in what you are saying.

h. *Your client is quitting her job next week to take a job elsewhere, but she can't tell anyone.* I have had this happen to me many times. I leave the call thinking, "Something is going on, but I don't quite know what it is." A month later when my client resigns, I find out what it was.

i. *Your client does not deal with salespeople frequently and does not know how to handle closing techniques.* This happens a lot with people who are in a buying position for the first time. I recommend that you do whatever it takes to stop acting like a salesperson.

10. Ask questions so that she will be motivated to answer them.

I believe the real key to getting a defensive client to drop the wall and get involved in your selling dialogue is to ask good questions. Your selling dialogue with a defensive client has to start on her turf, not yours. The only way you're going to get the dialogue onto her turf is for her to answer some questions. Sometimes clients are nervous about answering questions for fear of what might happen, but as *60 Minutes* correspondent Mike Wallace is fond of saying, "There are no indiscreet questions, only indiscreet answers."

Some tips:

a. *Prepare.* The more interesting a client finds your question-and-answer session, the longer it will last. If you bore your client by starting out at too basic a level, you will lose her quickly. The kinds of questions you ask reveal a lot about you. With preparation you can ask questions that are more on her level and hold her interest.

b. *Make conversation, not interrogation.* Your client is under no obligation to respond to even one of your questions. Some questions can be viewed as intrusive. A badly framed question can put a client on the defensive. Good questioners don't make the client feel uncomfortable or defensive.

c. *Ask new questions by bringing up your client's answers to earlier questions.* This is a way you can let the client know that you are really paying attention. "Marlene, earlier in our conversation you mentioned that you are trying to make more plastic worms. Have you considered adding a second production line?"

d. *Go from the general to the specific.* If you want the session to seem like a conversation, see that it flows like one. Conversation flows logically; it doesn't jump around. It is to your advantage to make the questioning technique invisible to your client and make the questions gently flow from the general to the specific.

e. *Really listen to the answers.* God gave us one mouth and two ears. If you listen twice as much as you talk you will be much smarter. People like to talk. They find it flattering to state their opinions and have someone carefully listen to them.

f. *Save sensitive questions for later in the interview.* If you save the sensitive questions until your client feels more comfortable with your questioning, the questions will get a much better reception.

g. *Take notes.* If you have a really good question-and-answer session, your client is going to share lots of great information. If you don't take notes you will forget some of it. The client who willingly answers your questions on this call may frown at answering the same questions the next time you visit.

h. *Ask open-ended questions.* The best sales calls are the ones where your customers do most of the talking. If you ask open-ended questions, they'll tell you about their business, they'll tell you what their problems are, and maybe they'll even tell you how your product already solves those problems.

Closing Strategies

If you can get your client to open up and start talking, your close will be like any other. If you go through your call and still get no feedback, then you have to close with no feedback. Try some of these pointers:

1. Close on your client's demographics.

Think to yourself, "OK, this woman works for a midsize company and is only moderately involved in my type of product. Typically, clients who are in this demographic position are looking for. . . ." I basically work toward the close on instinct and a radar pattern constructed from previous encounters with clients of similar demographics.

2. Time the close with no feedback.

If you get no feedback from the client, then just time the close to your pace, not hers. Usually you ask for the order when you are getting signals from the client that she is ready to buy, but if there is no feedback, work with your own sense of timing. When you feel that you have talked enough about your product, directly ask for the order.

3. Use the canned pitch close.

With a client who clams up you both lose. The client loses out because the real time customization she should be getting deteriorates into little more than a canned pitch. But every canned pitch has a canned close. Use it.

16

The Client Who
Knows It All

From the Tough Calls survey:

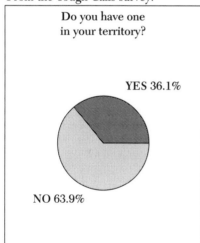

Do you have one
in your territory?

YES 36.1%

NO 63.9%

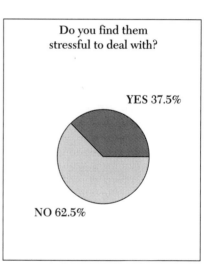

Do you find them
stressful to deal with?

YES 37.5%

NO 62.5%

"The customer is always sure they are right no matter what you tell them. You need to make sure they feel that way when you close the deal, even if they are idiots."

Sales and Marketing Manager, broadcast equipment,
Philadelphia, Pa.

She is brilliant, knowledgeable, and confident. She knows more about the product you sell than you will ever know and reminds you of this constantly on your call. When you try to push for a sale, she turns into an expertise bully who will use her knowledge and intellect to deflect any persuasive arguments you have.

She is used to being right about most things and has a hard time changing her mind, but to sell her for the first time this is exactly what you must do.

Giving her a presentation can be a nightmare, since she will pick apart every point you make while offering you advice on how your company should be doing things. Sometimes it is just very difficult to be persuasive with someone who knows so much more than you do. The first step in selling a know-it-all is to just get her to listen to you. Know-it-alls like to talk and have a harder time listening. Until you have earned their respect or gotten their attention, you can assume that they have not really heard a word you have said.

Pitfalls

1. Acting like a salesperson.

Know-it-alls often consider themselves to be too smart to sit through a sales presentation. Obviously, manipulative closing techniques like "Would you like a red one or a blue one?" will offend them. Don't be overly gratuitous or falsely enthusiastic. Going into a canned pitch is suicide, for if you come off like a common salesperson they will not listen to anything you have to say. In addition, they are often smart enough to know that many of the salespeople who call on them make more money and know far less than they do. Some know-it-alls not only do not listen to salesy types, they resent them.

2. Not preparing.

Know-it-alls are impressed with information. Before you visit one, you need to have your facts straight. Know-it-alls are bored with most salespeople; if you show up and have a conversation about the basics of their business you will lose them. You simply have to start the call at a higher level. Do some extra homework and understand completely what their business is like before you walk through the door.

3. Trying to compete with her expertise.

She is not buying from you, and she taps her vast experience to tell you why not. Your job is to convince her that she should buy, but if you question her expertise along the way, you are looking for trouble. She has invested years in becoming the expert on the scene. Somehow you have to be persuasive while still letting her be the expert.

4. Being intimidated.

If you start to get intimidated because you're calling on someone who knows so much more than you do, just remember: Your job is to motivate a sale, not to match wits. You do not need to know as much as she does to accomplish this. Sometimes knowing too much can actually get in the way.

Selling Strategies

1. Don't be impressive; be impressed.

Ask yourself, "Emotionally why did this client spend so much time becoming an expert?" No one becomes an expertise bully just by sliding through school or reading a few trade journals. There is real motivation at play here, and if you can tap into it, you can often move a sale along. Know-it-alls love to demonstrate their expertise, they love to command respect and admiration, and in many cases the admiration is well deserved. So extend it and acknowledge their expertise.

I once had a big problem with one of the brightest and most knowledgeable clients I have ever called on. I had really been looking forward to meeting with him. Because I pride myself on being somewhat of an expert in the industry we were both in, I thought we would hit it off immediately. When we started talking I found we were just not clicking, though. I just could not get him to buy from me. Finally, it occurred to me that what he really wanted was not a peer, but an audience. I changed my whole approach and just listened to what he had to say. And from that point on, the more I showed up and just listened to him with wide-eyed amazement, the more he bought from me.

2. Become a conduit for expertise.

If you really have to get into the details of your product to make a sale and this level of detail is over your head, try this. Level with her, tell her that her expertise is much greater than that of the typical client you call on, but you think her feedback is vital for your organization to hear, not just because you want to make a sale, but because it is so extraordinary that it will enhance future product development. Take out a notepad and ask her to share everything she has to say about why she is not buying your product. Take lots of notes, then retreat from the field of battle with your honor still intact. When you get back to your office go over your client's feedback point by point. Discuss it with your management or perhaps with a product expert. Arrange a second call with your client, and when you get in tell her you are going to respond in detail with the full expertise of people in your organization to every point she made.

About half the time I have done this, clients loved it. They found it flattering to be taken so seriously, and the people at my company came up with some terrific responses that the client had never considered. These people really did have a passion for their companies and products, and lived for the details. However, I have had other clients who lost interest almost immediately in the presentation after I responded to just the first few points that they had made. These clients had far less passion for the product detail and loved to be the experts more for the ego trip it afforded them. Either way, though, this approach was a success from a sales point of view. For the people with passion for details, the call really sold them. For the people who use their expertise only as an ego trip, pinning down the details stopped them from being an expertise bully and got them back into a selling dialogue.

3. Have her critique your next presentation.

Know-it-alls almost never sit still for a presentation; they will disagree with every point and often tell you how you really should be giving this presentation. Why not give them a chance to do just that? Make them one of the first people who see a new presentation; show it to them less as a client and more as a consultant. Tell them, "I have a new presentation and I want

to show it to you for feedback before I show it to anyone else."
Know-it-alls love this, and while they help you make your presentation better, they have to take your point of view, at least for
the moment. The other reason to do this is that you often come
away with a much better presentation.

4. Give her a five-idea presentation.

Stop trying to sell her with information, which will not impress
her since she knows it all anyway, and instead sell her with
ideas. If your ideas are original, this presentation can have a real
impact. An idea that your client has not heard before begs for
her vast knowledge to help in its implementation.

Call her up and acknowledge that she is the great expert,
but tell her that you have five ideas that may intrigue her. You
can't base your presentation around just one idea because if
your client has already heard of it or does not like it, you're
sunk. Sometimes what you are doing is just repackaging your
sales presentation more in terms of ideas and less in terms of
statistics or facts. Again, you may have to talk to people at the
home office to come up with five truly original ideas, but if you
tap into the knowledge of everyone in your organization who
might have one, you can often come up with some original ones.
If you can show her five ideas that will integrate your product
into her buying patterns to save money, make money, improve
operations, and so on, you can often intrigue the know-it-all.

5. Get help from the one expert your client will listen to: herself.

Some know-it-alls place a far greater importance on their point
of view than is realistic. Their view is not just the view of another ordinary person, it is *the* view of one of the enlightened
few. Very often the only one who can change their mind about
things is themselves. One way to sell them is to crawl into their
point of view and sell them from within. Here is how you do
this:

Ask your client to talk about the subject she knows best and
loves to talk about: her area of expertise. As one favorite editor
of mine likes to say, "Ask him a few questions, stand back, and
let him blow." Know-it-alls love to talk and talk and talk. Use

this naturally occurring resource to help your client give you detailed access to her point of view. While she talks and talks and talks about her business, you are doing three things.

First, you are actively listening for selling opportunities. If you sell buttons and hear that your client is about to begin a new line of Chinese silk pajamas, tell her about your buttons that would fit into the new line. If you sell electrical conduit, ask about new buildings they may be putting up and tell her about your new line of conduit that incorporates voice and data wiring. If you sell pharmaceutical product and hear that the drugstore chain you are calling on is opening a new store in Florida, tell her about the kinds of products you carry that clients in the South typically stock. Some clients will be too guarded at first to share these kinds of opportunities with you; it might take a while to build a sense of trust that would lead to this kind of dialogue. Sometimes future plans may be somewhat confidential.

Second, you are actively listening for her own statements that you can paraphrase back to her to move the conversation in a way that may uncover a selling opportunity. "Joan, earlier in our conversation you mentioned that you might be expanding your operations. Can you tell me more about those plans?"

Third, you are moving the conversation along through the use of questions. "Joan, could you share your thoughts on the trend by some clothing designers to use highly decorative buttons on plain clothes designs?" Throughout this process you do not overtly suggest any buying activity; you question. You do not overtly direct the conversation; you invite comment. You do not overtly sell her; you help her try out new buying ideas until she finds one that fits. You are turning your call into a working laboratory where you pretty much give up most of the control of the call to your client's point of view and slowly steer the conversation to a point where your client will buy from you.

To do all this you need a) a real interest in your client's business, b) the patience to listen to a lot of information that will not directly lead to a sale, c) a genuine willingness to get to know your client's point of view so that you can opportunistically integrate your product into her view, and d) a commitment of time to accomplish all this when there might be other clients you can simply close sooner with much less effort.

6. Dig deep and find a piece of information your client does not know.

There is no better way to start off a call with a know-it-all than by offering a piece of information that she did not know before. Know-it-alls love information, and obscure bits of information fascinate them: a cute story about how her company was founded or a personal bit of information about her company's CEO or president, information about how her company does with certain overseas operations. You can get these by reviewing annual reports, buying stock in the company and getting company updates, or just by doing some basic library research. Starting a call this way accomplishes several things with a know-it-all. It gets her attention, it gives you credibility, and it will impress her to the point where she will listen to you.

7. Prove your product's worth to her with her own involvement in a special project.

If you can channel a know-it-all's expertise into a special project, you can often fascinate her with something that can also demonstrate the value of your product. I once sold a know-it-all by conducting a survey of his company's customers. While we developed the questionnaire, my client had the opportunity to expound on all kinds of things. In the questionnaire we also asked how his customers felt about the product I was trying to sell him. He got very interested in the survey, and when it came back that my product was highly valued among his customers, he bought from me big time. If you don't work in a product category where a survey is appropriate, see whether you can get a know-it-all to help your organization develop new product ideas, new packaging or pricing designs, or a new dealer incentive plan before they are cast in stone.

8. Send long follow-up letters.

Know-it-alls are often fanatical readers; thus the written word often has more selling power with these kinds of clients. A well-written follow-up letter that goes into a lot of detail can often get more of their attention than a personal call.

9. *Make a joint call with a company expert.*

Sometimes it's just easier to bring along your own expert. If you can bring along a field engineer or a product expert from the home office on your next call to this know-it-all, you can often make big points. After a plant tour and twenty minutes of shop talk, very often the expertise bully will look more favorably upon your proposals.

10. *Establish common ground on a different level.*

I once called on a horrific expertise bully. He just kept talking and talking and talking. It was like a filibuster. I just couldn't get a word in edgewise. The thing that broke the filibuster and moved the sale along was doing something personal for him. I found out that he had a hobby of collecting ties. I started a call by giving him a tie that was particularly hard to find. He was very touched by this personal gesture, shut his mouth, and motioned me to sit down and present my story. He didn't say a single word until I had completed my presentation, after which he started to become a customer.

11. *Ask yourself, "What if she only thinks she is an expert?"*

Some know-it-alls really don't know that much and aren't really so brilliant or insightful; they only think they are. If you notice that your client just doesn't have her facts straight or comes to obviously incorrect conclusions in your conversations, you may be dealing with one of these nonexpert know-it-alls. Often these people are very knowledgeable in their trained area of expertise, but they have been promoted into areas where they just don't know that much. I once sold ad space for an engineering magazine. I would often call on brilliant engineers who had built thriving technology companies, but there is little in the training, expertise, and experience of engineers that equips them to buy advertising space. However, I assure you that I had no shortage of "advertising experts" to call on. I find that in many cases these people genuinely appreciate your help if you can give it to them in a way that lets them save face. Never tell them they are wrong; always give them an alternative way to look at things, and offer to explain things in a way they have never heard of before. On some level these folks seem to realize that they don't know as much as they would like to present. Very often if you give them a face-saving way to follow your lead, they will.

Closing Strategies

1. Get her to evaluate a different point of view.

Usually you cannot change a know-it-all's point of view immediately. If you are persuasive and can get her to consider an alternative point of view, leave her office and come back in a week. She may then volunteer, "You know that other point of view we talked about? Well, I've done some thinking. . . ." She may embellish your proposal, she may change it around completely, but somehow she has adapted it as her own idea and therefore it's OK.

2. Tie your product to her product on a detailed level.

Here the sale is motivated by some compatible details that you have uncovered in your sales call.

3. Have her close herself.

Here you ask leading questions that logically lead to a close. See Chapter 17 for more details on this approach.

4. Become her friend and ask for the order.

Sometimes the least obvious way to close a know-it-all is the best. I know of one know-it-all who is unquestionably brilliant and knows his company and products better than anyone. However, he is extremely arrogant and has no friends. The salespeople who befriended him got his business.

5. Get her out of the abstract and into the concrete.

If your client talks about her business all day, she will never buy. Ask direct questions that get her out of the abstract world of her business and into the concrete world of buying or not buying your product. Sometimes she will raise all kinds of off-the-wall abstract objections that you have never heard of before. Many know-it-alls have this egghead mentality and do this as an intellectual exercise. Use your judgment, but often the best approach is to ignore the objections and reassert your need for a commitment.

6. *Let her be the big expert so that she will let you have the big order.*

Know-it-alls have an emotional need to feel intellectually superior to the people who are calling on them. Sometimes the primary "objection" with a client like this is that you have not sufficiently acknowledged her superiority in her field. Her ego may be very tied to hearing this kind of feedback, so acknowledge her expertise and ask for the order.

17

The Client Who
Is an Egomaniac

From the Tough Calls survey:

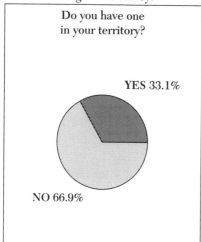

Do you have one
in your territory?

YES 33.1%

NO 66.9%

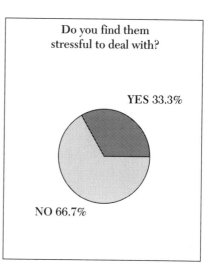

Do you find them
stressful to deal with?

YES 33.3%

NO 66.7%

*"It's a problem you cannot logically deal with. You must grovel
or use psychology."*

Marketing Manager, golf accessories, Portland, Oreg.

The most direct path to sell an egomaniac is through his ego,
but in sales large egos are very delicate and dangerous things. I
think of selling an egomaniac as selling a client with a very large
angry bear sitting right beside him in the room. The client will
do whatever the bear will do, but the bear is difficult to control.
The bear gets dangerous with any kind of provocation or sud-

den movement. The bear does not respond to logic or intelligent communications, but it can often be led around the room with handfuls of raisins or a pot of honey brought along with you for the occasion.

I am constantly surprised at how many perfectly normal, psychologically healthy people turn into egomaniacs when you give them the power to buy products or services. But not all egomaniacs are made; some are born. The job of buying sometimes attracts egomaniacs. Where else can someone of average ability attract a flock of admiring fans all wanting to please, entertain, and praise as long as he controls the budget?

Pitfalls

1. Not figuring out that he is an egomaniac before the close.

In the movies egomaniacs are easy to spot. They have loud ties, have loud voices, and come from Brooklyn; but in business, blatant ego-driven behavior is often frowned upon and business egomaniacs are driven underground. But when you push for a close, surprise! You've discovered that there's just a lot of ego-related ground you needed to cover, and you could be much farther from a sale than you thought. The best way to deal with an egomaniac is to spot him early. Here are some clues:

   a. *The desk.* Egomaniacs who have control over their office design often have unusual desks. I have called on egomaniacs with an oversized desk, a Louis XIV antique desk, a desk on a raised platform, a desk with a flag of the United States on one side and the state of Massachusetts flag on the other, a desk designed to be under a skylight that illuminated it by day, and a glass-top desk. A desk is the control console from which an egomaniac operates. He will often have some kind of custom design in the desk made just for him.
   b. *"Me" kinds of things on the walls.* What a client chooses to decorate his office with is a sure sign of the kind of person he is. Clients can have a variety of things on their

walls: They could have pictures of their family, company memorabilia, or items about themselves. The "me" office has lots of things of this nature; awards that he won, a picture of "me" with the President of the United States, a picture of "me" with Albert Einstein, and so on.

   c. *Lots of "I" talk.* You know this the minute you walk in the room. The client talks about "I" like this and "I" like that and "I" think this is great, and so on, and so forth. He talks more about himself and less about his business.

2. Getting into an argument.

Egomaniacs have strong opinions and express them openly. Often in the first sales visit they may tell you why they don't buy your product and what they don't like about it. But unlike most clients, these kinds of statements are not expressed to elicit a dialogue; they are expressed to "tell you how things are." The egomaniac always has to be right. Disagreeing with him is very dangerous. Instead, listen carefully to criticisms he might have for your product, and find a nonconfrontational way to respond. Also, I recommend sidestepping any strongly expressed opinion that does not directly affect the sale of your product. In sales your job is to change the point of view of people who are not buying from you, but you cannot win an argument with an egomaniac. You cannot get the bear angry, but you can lead him.

3. Trying to use a trial close with him.

Generally, asking for the order early in the selling process is a good technique for flushing out objections so that you can deal with them more quickly. But using this routine sales technique on an egomaniac can backfire. Egomaniacs always have to be right, and if they were right about not wanting to buy your product early in the call, by golly, they're going to be right until the bitter end. It is best not to press an egomaniac for a decisive answer until you have made all the persuasive points you have to make. Once an egomaniac tells you no, it is very hard to get him to say yes later on.

Selling Strategies

1. Make him think it was his idea.

Who owns the idea to buy your proposal? If it is your idea, you
lose. You have to get the egomaniac to own the idea of buying
from you. Then he will fight for it. Here are the steps:

  a. *First float the idea by him; mention the buying idea in passing.*
     "Some of my customers are buying in lots of six to save
     money on the shipping." Or you can bring up the idea
     more directly by asking a question: "Have you ever con-
     sidered that if you buy in lots of six you can save a lot of
     money on shipping?" You must float the question very
     subtly, because eventually you are going to give full
     credit for the idea to your client—and the less clearly he
     remembers you bringing up the idea in the first place,
     the better.
  b. *Get a reaction.* Hopefully he will react to your idea, al-
     though sometimes you have to float the idea past a few
     times in different ways until he reacts. In one situation I
     rephrased my idea three different ways, then finally
     asked a direct question before I got my client to notice.
     He might react like this, "Lots of six—do you really
     think there's that much savings?" You might then explain
     that it costs only a little bit more to ship six than it does
     to ship one, so there is tremendous savings involved.
  c. *Get the idea adapted.* Your client may note that his factory
     creates his product in lots of four, but that's OK because
     there is still a big savings. Here the idea gets adapted
     slightly so that it fits into your customer's situation: in
     the example I'm using, not shipping in lots of six as you
     proposed, but in lots of four.
  d. *Label it as his.* Label the adaptation as a whole new idea
     and give him full credit for it. You say, "Hey that's a great
     idea you had, shipping in lots of four." If someone else
     walks into the room you might say, "Mark just came up
     with a terrific idea. Do you realize if you ship your prod-
     uct in lots of four it will save your company big money
     on the shipping?"

I know this sounds corny when you explain it, and you might ask, "Don't these people realize that they didn't come up with the original idea?" I have never had an egomaniac call me on it. Such clients are happy to take full credit for any good idea that comes their way, and once they have identified it as their own idea, they will fight for its implementation.

2. Use questions to lead him through selling points.

Earlier I mentioned leading the bear with a pot of honey. The pot of honey is asking questions, and egomaniacs love answering questions. Since expressing opinions is what they do best, answering questions is pure flattery. Openly disagreeing with an egomaniac is dangerous, but you can lead the client through your sales approach through questioning. For example, if you are dealing with an egomaniac who has never bought red gumdrops from you, you might ask the following questions:

You: Right now you buy only green gumdrops, right?

Client: Yes, we've been buying green gumdrops for many years.

You: Have you ever considered any other color of gumdrop?

Client: From time to time we have, but we always come back to green. It has worked the best over the years for us.

You: You mentioned that you have tried other colors of gumdrops. Which ones?

Client: We looked at orange, we tried yellow once, but no one liked the flavor. Our tasters just couldn't get over the yellow flavor.

You: Have you ever tried red?

Client: No, we never have.

You: What would persuade you to try red gumdrops?

Client: Actually, we have never considered it.

> *You:*   If I could arrange for a sample to be shipped to
>   your tasters, would you have them give them
>   a try?
>
> *Client:*   Sure, why not? I am always open to new things.

You use the questions to flush out points, then you build on them. In this case we discovered that it is the tasters at this man's organization who have ruled out buying red gumdrops in the past. You have to listen very carefully for points that lead in the direction you want them to go in, and then build on them to frame the next questions.

3. Appeal to his sense of fair play.

In any disagreement there are several points of view, but the egomaniac always thinks that his side is right. This may be problematic in dealing with him in many ways, but one benefit to you is that most egomaniacs truly believe that they are extremely fair and honest—after all, how could they not be? They're always right. If you are on the outside of an account, you can often get an appointment to present a different point of view by appealing to an egomaniac's sense of fair play.

4. Ask him, "How should I sell you?"

Many clients hearing this would ask you why they should tell you any such thing: "Why should I do your job for you?" But egomaniacs will often find it flattering: They're not just telling you how they buy the kinds of products you sell, they think they are telling you how everyone in the universe should be buying your products. As they are explaining this to you, they might add that they know the right way to buy and anyone else who does it differently is not quite up to snuff. Some clients may think you presumptuous to ask this question. Egomaniacs will take it as flattery.

5. Sell to his value system first, to his company second.

As a salesperson representing a product, you are more than just a mouthpiece. How you behave on the call is also being evaluated. Since many egomaniacs make buying decisions on instinct and not product details, how you present yourself personally can have tremendous impact. Often egomaniacs have strong ideas about the right way to call on them. I have sold egomaniacs who have told me, "There are no excuses for showing up late, and any salesperson who shows up late in my office is a loser whom I don't have to do business with." Another told me, "Any salesperson who calls on me who has dirty fingernails is not worth talking to." Another told me, "I would never buy from a sales rep who is overweight. If he can't control his weight, how can he control the details of my account?" Egomaniacs can sometimes have crazy ideas about how you should and should not act on a call, so it's important to find out how an egomaniac wants you to approach him on the call. With most clients, you position your product according to the business needs of the company, but with this client it's almost always important to sell the ego managing the account. You might ask, "How do you like to work with salespeople like me who call on you?"

6. If you get stuck, ask him about his favorite subject: himself.

Egomaniacs love to talk about themselves. Ask the right questions and stand back and watch them blow. Ask, "How long have you been with this company?" Or, "How did you get started as a pharmaceutical product buyer?" Ask about any personal memorabilia on the walls of his office.

7. Use flattery, even if it's corny.

Egomaniacs love themselves and think everyone else should too. They love flattery, to them there is no finer sound. Overt flattery may sound corny to you and may sound corny to many of your more psychologically adjusted clients, but to egomaniacs it is what they live for.

8. Make it look like a lot of work.

Egomaniacs love to think that you are working very hard to get their business, since they think that they are so important and that their business should take center stage when it comes time to sell them. Always mention to the egomaniac just how many extra hours you've spent on his account, how many times you went back to your boss to get an extra concession. Make him feel that you are working for him.

Closing Strategies

1. Give him a chance to use his power to buy.

The egomaniac takes great pride in the power he wields when he buys. If you can create a theatrical setting for him to demonstrate his power, you can often motivate him to buy on the spot. As you lead up to the close, understand what he is capable of buying within his budget, and ask for an order that you know he can accept. If possible, ask for the order when other people are in the room, especially subordinates who report to him. Phrase the final question in terms of how he has the opportunity to buy, and whether he would like to do it. For example, "Ralph, I know you've considered long and hard the choices you have open to you. Right now you are the only one who can make this decision. What will it be?"

2. Have him close himself.

This is the logical extension of selling strategy number 2 of using questions to lead through selling points. If you use questions to get him through all the selling points that you have, the logical last question you should ask is, "Can I have the order?"

3. Let him save face if he buys from you.

There is no client who needs more face-saving devices presented to him at the time of the close than the egomaniac. If he was not buying your product in the past and is to now start buying it, the question is, was he in error in the past? The answer can never be yes, so somehow you have to come up with a rationale as to how things have changed so that not buying in the past was right and buying now in the present is also right. For more tips on how to do this, check Closing Strategies in Chapter 10.

18

The Client Who Gets Angry Over Mix-Ups

From the Tough Calls survey:

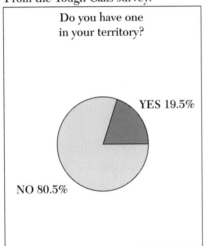

Do you have one in your territory?

YES 19.5%

NO 80.5%

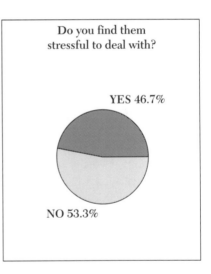

Do you find them stressful to deal with?

YES 46.7%

NO 53.3%

"Stay calm no matter how worked up the client gets."
Sales Manager, marketing services company, Costa Mesa, Calif.

Mistakes happen, problems come up, and most clients understand this. But there are some problematic clients who prey on these situations and play hardball to extract significant concessions. However, I know some master salespeople who routinely turn these potential train wrecks into increased business. For them a major problem is like a high-stakes poker game where there is the opportunity to significantly increase business with a client or lose it all.

In politics the "defining moment" is an event when the nebulous public image of a new politician is crystallized in the national conscience. In sales your "defining moment," in the eyes of a client, comes when a big problem arises. When a big problem comes up, your client is focused on you and your company as at no other time. With a problematic client an unstoppable chain of events gets put into motion. An honest mistake becomes a scene. Great lengths are gone through to make the error look more damaging than it is, and massive concessions are demanded.

Problems are both a curse and a blessing. Solving them is the most important thing you do.

Pitfalls

1. Not trying to use it to your advantage.

I know what it is like to get those angry phone calls. They come out of the blue, and suddenly you are being yelled at for someone else's mistake. Through no fault of your own, your client is livid and threatening to pull all of his business. These phone calls are particularly painful on an account where you have personally spent extra time and effort.

But consider the opportunity that a major problem presents. Suddenly everyone who can make a difference on the account is paying extreme attention. Your client, his boss, and your boss are suddenly taking a break from the routine to focus their attention on the details of this situation. In the process of explaining the damage done, your client often shares more information than usual about how his company does things. Your boss will likely grant you permission to give concessions that go beyond the routine. More attention and substantive efforts will come from both sides. By taking charge of this (hopefully) brief and intense event, you have the opportunity to change your relationship with this client for months to come.

2. Letting the problem linger for longer than it has to.

When a problem comes up, your client is thinking negatively about you and your company. Don't let him stew in this negative mode for long. The faster you can resolve this, the faster you can get your client to thinking about you in positive terms. Do whatever it takes to bring this to resolution as quickly as possible.

3. Getting defensive and blaming it on the guy in shipping or production.

While doing this may take the heat off of you personally, it reflects badly on your company. Your client doesn't care that it's the fault of the guy in shipping who got fired last week. Ultimately it is your organization's product that you sell. If your organization looks mixed up, it will be harder for you to get follow-up orders. Instead of singling out an individual, tell him in specific, nonjudgmental terms why the problem occurred and why it will not happen again. Present your organization as a team that learns from its mistakes.

4. Asking your boss to handle it.

Your importance is about to be defined in your client's eyes. If you are the one who can be relied upon to solve problems when they come up, you will be looked at as a valuable resource. If you are the person who just takes the orders and is nowhere around when problems come up, you will be perceived as having very low value.

First of all, take full, personal responsibility for solving the problem from your side of the equation. If possible, see that you are the only one your client needs to talk to at your company to resolve the problem. You may have to do some tap dancing internally to do this, but the respect you will earn from your client during this critical passage will make it worth it. If you pass the buck to your manager, your value in the eyes of the client will be greatly diminished.

Selling Strategies

1. Defuse the anger.

Before you can do anything, you have to get your client to stop yelling at you. Sometimes letting your client vent anger is helpful, but beyond a point the yelling has to stop and the problem solving has to start. If your client will just will not calm down, try one of these:

a. *Tell him, "You're right."* If he is right, tell him so. Most often clients keep yelling when they think you are arguing with them or at least not agreeing. It is hard to keep confronting someone who is offering nothing to confront.

b. *Ask him for details of the problem.* This often gets the client out of the yelling mode and into a problem-solving mode. Asking for details invites him to pause and concentrate on smaller things, to explain them. Have you ever tried to yell a lot of small details at someone?

c. *Make a personal commitment to solve the problem.* If your client thinks this problem is a big deal, make sure you react to it as if it is a big deal. Tell him that you are on the case and that you will see that it gets handled.

d. *Tell him, "Hold on, I'll be right over."* If practical, drop what you are doing and visit the client as soon as possible. It is hard to yell at someone who just made a quick trip over and is sitting in your office; it is far easier to yell for long periods of time over the phone.

e. *Ask how he would like to see this resolved.* Here again you are inviting him into problem-solving mode.

2. Get him to talk it out.

Client anger can drive a lot of information your way in a short span of time. You need to listen for the substance of the complaint, but also for the emotional side of the complaint—that is, just how mad is he? Sometimes the client just wants an acknowledgment that something got loused up, and he simply needs to blow off steam.

But it is not enough to listen passively. You need to listen actively, ask questions, and pump for more details because you have some important things to find out. The more you can get your client to talk about his misfortune, the more likely you are to find out what you need to resolve the situation positively. By encouraging your client to talk, you are also sending a reassuring message that you really do want to resolve the problem favorably. While actively listening, you should be reading the client for the following things:

    a. What kind of concessions those at his company might
       be expecting
    b. What kind of concessions they might find valuable
    c. How strongly they value the product you provide
    d. How much value they put on their relationship with you
    e. How angry they are
    f. Specifically who is really angry

3. Find the "magic bullet" concession.

When a big problem comes up, there is a lot of top-down pressure on all parties to get the best for their organization. Your boss and your client's boss are paying careful attention. Finding a magic bullet concession takes advantage of this. Here is how it works: Your boss as sales manager is under pressure to minimize revenue loss and maximize future sales. Your client needs to get compensation for any inconvenience or lost business, but since his boss is probably watching him, what he really needs is to get the biggest concession package possible.

If this process is not managed, it will typically deteriorate straight to a demand for cash off the current order, and both sides lose. Your boss, under pressure to minimize revenue loss, will grant a meager settlement, and your client, who needs to look good in front of his boss, will look terrible. Everyone is going to be very miserable, especially you. The solution is to come up with a concession that has more cash value for your client than for your company and that might give your company an advantage for future sales opportunities.

After you have listened carefully to what your client has to say, go back to your boss and talk turkey. Come up with a concession package that benefits your company's needs first. For example:

- Give a concession that lets the client try a product he has not used before.
- Give a concession that is doled out over time so as to guarantee future business on a regular basis.
- Give a concession that lets your client experience the benefits of using your product at higher levels of volume, in hope that they get used to it.
- Give a concession that helps get acceptance of a new product that your company is introducing.
- Give a concession that has special meaning for the client personally.

The best of these concession ideas come from the details of how your customer uses your products and how you go to market. The concession gives your client more involvement in your company and its products.

You might think that I am advocating acting only in the best interest of your company, but this is absolutely not true. What your client needs above all else is to show his boss that he got the biggest concession package possible. He will get the maximum only when there is some extra benefit for your organization.

4. Sell the magic bullet concession.

First off, you have to sell your boss on this concession package. Without your boss you have nothing. The idea is to give things away that will build more business eventually between you and your client. Then you have to sell the concession package to your client. Too often these packages are not about what is fair and reasonable compensation for inconvenience or damage done. In problem situations more often these boil down to a test of power as to how much can be extracted out of your organization. But most of the time it is more about politics than substance. Very often it is not how much the client gets out of you, but how much it *looks* as if he gets out of you. What you have to do is to sell the relevant people at his company on the idea that they got a heck of a deal and that they came out way ahead. Some tips:

a. Establish a benchmark. What is appropriate compensation for this kind of mix-up? By giving them a benchmark to measure their concession against, you can help them understand the value of what they got. Describe for them a similar situation where a problem arose and a concession was granted.

b. Compare the dollar value of what they lost in the mix-up to how much they got in concessions.

c. If this is a concession based on the personal preferences of your client, let him know that he is getting it because of your personal understanding of his or his company's needs.

If the settlement is not adequate, ask the client what he feels would be a fair settlement. Buried in the response to this question is the answer to another question: Just how serious does your client think this problem is, and just how upset are those at his company?

5. Ask what the client wants.

Some clients know exactly what they want and will tell you. If their requests are reasonable, the problem will pass quickly. The tricky part of using this technique is that they may ask for things that are unreasonable. If you ask, and they tell you, and then you have to go back and tell them it is unacceptable, you have shot yourself in the foot. (If their demands are excessive, see Selling Strategy 10 later in this chapter.)

6. Stay on top of this situation until it is resolved.

Maintain constant contact with the client, even if you have nothing of substance to say, until the whole matter is resolved. Call and say, "Look, I called my boss, and she is still working to find out what went wrong. We should know by tomorrow. I don't have any news, but I want you to know we are working on your problem." The emotional message you are sending is: "I care, I'm on your side, I'll fix this."

7. Run interference.

Once again, no matter how the solution to the problem plays itself out, make sure that you are the key person in its resolution.

Don't let your client's hands get dirty dealing with problematic people inside your organization. If your operations director has the personality of Frankenstein, handle the internal details for the client. Take charge. If you can make yourself the only person he has to deal with to resolve things, you will be far more important in the client's mind for all future dealings you have with him.

8. If you can, take a preemptive strike.

The best way for a client to hear about a problem that is caused by your organization is from you. As soon as you find out that there is a problem, rush to find some details about what happened and then rush to a phone. You can make big, big points by calling your client first. The whole psychological dynamic changes. Suddenly you are not defensively hearing about news; you are proactively taking charge and doing something about it. The emotional message it sends is one that inspires confidence. It says, "We are on top of things. We made a mistake, but we know about it and are fixing it."

9. Write a letter.

If the situation is complex, document the problem in a letter from you to your boss with a copy to the client.

10. "Help! I've done everything right, but the client is still mad."

You have listened, you've paid attention, you have offered concessions. And yet your client is still not happy. You need to offer more. Some possibilities:

a. *Love.* Some problem situations get taken personally. At one small family-run business the people just could not get past the fact that we had made a mistake on their account. Weeks after I thought the matter was resolved, they still had to talk about it. I had my boss and my boss's boss call on them at an industry event. We offered some terrific concessions. But they were still mad. It was not until I took them out for a family dinner that they got past it. Emotionally they took our mistake as an assault on their family, and it took a family gathering for them to finally forgive us.

Sometimes it is the emotional side that gets way out of hand. Small, struggling businesses can see errors as very threatening. Growing, passionate businesses take errors very personally. Family-run businesses can take them as marks as much against their family as their business. In these situations, personal gestures can mean as much as big concessions that play more to the logical side.

This is how I think about coming up with an appropriate personal gesture: I imagine that my client is my best friend and that I have just made a mistake that caused him great personal pain. What would you do? What would you say, and how would you say it? You might send a gift that has personal meaning, make a personal visit, do some personal entertaining, or make it up to him in some personal way.

b. *Blood*. Every territory has a few accounts that you just pray nothing goes wrong with. When something does, it is like a game of Monopoly when you land on Park Place just after your opponent has put a hotel on it. "Why me, why him?" you ask. He calls you up and blasts you on the phone, demands unreasonable concessions, and threatens to pull all his business if he does not get what he wants immediately.

Understand the theater of the situation. He may be mad, and maybe legitimately so. One reason he is yelling is that he cannot view this as a routine problem. If this is a routine problem, then it is very possible that he made a terrible decision to buy from you. But if he can tell his boss that you were shocked and amazed and bent over backward to accommodate, suddenly he will look better in the eyes of his boss.

Maybe he is insecure and passing that on to you. Maybe his boss is an SOB. Maybe he is just being demanding to see how much he can get out of you. Maybe he has earned a reputation as someone who gets the best out of suppliers who make mistakes. Maybe he wants your organization to pay more careful attention to the details of his business. It doesn't matter why. What he is really after is "blood," loosely translated as a concession that goes beyond what is usual or painless. First offer a reasonable concession package and explain why this is typically how these things are resolved. Then offer an extra "blood" concession. The amazing thing is that the extra need not be a large concession, just as long as it is understood to be above and beyond.

c. *Attention.* When the yelling is about a bruised ego, your client might have a case of "title-itis." Noting you can do or say will satisfy. After all, you are the person who calls on him all the time. Attention from you is nothing special. If there is someone in your organization who has celebrity status or whom you know your client has tremendous respect for, have that person give a call and offer apologies. Sometimes the very same words just coming from someone else in your organization can make the difference.

d. *Political help.* How does this mistake reflect on the career of the person who bought from you? He bought from you, then your products or organization let him down, and now his judgment is being questioned by his boss. In one situation where there was a mistake caused by mutual confusion, I took full responsibility for the error, extended apologies to his boss, and told the boss what a great job the client was doing.

e. *Therapy.* Some clients really do not know what they want. They know they are unhappy, and they know they should be getting something out of you. The problem is that this kind of indecision can drag the settlement process on and on. But it is to your advantage for the settlement to be over quickly. Sit the client down, preferably in a face-to-face meeting, and ask, "What do you want?" Then offer a series of possibilities, discuss them, and help the client choose.

The other, less common client is the one who does not express the true degree of his dissatisfaction. Months later, after you thought the problem was well behind you it turns up again like a bad penny.

Closing Strategies

1. Use postproblem bonding.

In any close client relationship there will disagreements and problems. If you can resolve the difficulties to everyone's satisfaction, you often strengthen your relationship. The sunny after-glow of solving a tough problem together can be a time to talk about increasing business.

2. Use what you have learned to help you sell up.

During the process of working through the problem, you have probably gotten to know your client better. Take inventory. What have you learned? What did you learn about your client's business that will help you frame a new proposal to help sell up his business?

19

The Client Who
Is Incompetent

From the Tough Calls survey:

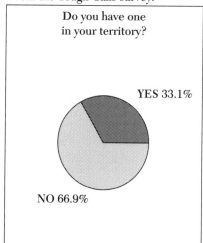

Do you have one
in your territory?

YES 33.1%

NO 66.9%

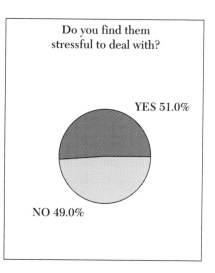

Do you find them
stressful to deal with?

YES 51.0%

NO 49.0%

*"The incompetent buyer does not know what he or she is buying
and will rarely buy the right product or know if they have been
taken. They simply photocopy a spec and bid it. Aggravating and
frustrating at best."*

Sales and Marketing Manager, broadcast equipment,
Philadelphia, Pa.

The call starts out fine, but after a while you notice that this
person is not asking the questions he should be asking and not
raising the kinds of objections that a client in his position typically raises. Some of the objections he does raise seem a little

off the wall, and you ask yourself, "Why is this person worried about these things?" After a time you realize this person does not know what he is doing; he is just going through the motions. The lights are on, but there is no one home.

I went on one call and it just seemed too easy. In the first five minutes the client told me, "I'm going to buy from you, I like your product, I like your company, I like the whole approach you take. I'm sold." I showed up, said almost nothing, walked away with the order, and all I could think was, "What happened?" Two months later, when I called on him again for a follow-up order, he told me he had just bought everything he needed from a direct competitor. I was stunned. When I asked why he did this, he told me that my product was out of date, and then went into a monologue that was taken practically word for word from my direct competitor's competitive selling promotions. I found out later that this direct competitor had taken him out on his yacht for an afternoon and sold him hook, line, and sinker. All I could think was, "What happened?" again.

Incompetent clients are everywhere. They do not buy the best value for their company, they do not ask the right questions, and they are not demanding when they could or should be. The scariest ones truly believe that they know exactly what they are doing. Sometimes people new to the buying experience get a swelled head, an exaggerated opinion of themselves and their ability to make buying judgments. All through college or when they had that job in shipping, they were nobody; then suddenly they are in a position to buy things, and people twice their age want to entertain them, meet with them, and hang on their every word.

Sometimes incompetent clients are an easy mark for a quick sale, but if any one word describes them, it is "unpredictable." In the world of prize fighting, the opponent many fear most is the one who is inexperienced, since he is often the one who is unpredictable, taking risks that a more experienced fighter would never dream of. I think of selling incompetent clients as a double-or-nothing proposition. Sometimes incompetent clients are the best clients you can have, who will give you a disproportionately high amount of their business even when it is not in their best interest to do so. Sometimes they are the worst, becoming a giant sinkhole where a lot of time and energy goes in and not much business comes out.

Pitfalls

1. Thinking clients are incompetent because they are not buying from you.

When you really believe in your product, it sometimes seems impossible that someone could buy from your competition and still be competent, let alone sane. You really do have to put your ego on hold and be objective. Just because a client is not buying your line does not mean he is incompetent. The real problem comes when salespeople use this as an excuse to stop working an account before they should. Your job is not to evaluate your client; it's to sell him.

2. Thinking of incompetence only as a negative.

Strictly from a selling point of view, client incompetence represents a selling opportunity. Extremely competent clients are not as needy and really don't need a lot of your help and often don't want a whole lot of your input. Incompetent clients are often the ones with whom you can make an honest difference. And there is nothing wrong with being an incompetent buyer. I have met many extremely bright and capable clients who got promoted into higher positions, where the buying decisions they had to make were simply beyond their level of expertise. Are they incompetent? Yes, when it comes to buying my product, but in many other areas that their organization places a much higher value on, they're on top of their game.

3. Forgetting that they are, in fact, the ones doing the buying.

Life can seem unfair: You may know more about your product than your client does, and you may even think you can do your client's job better than he does, but he is still the one doing the buying and you are still the one doing the selling.

4. Spending too much time with them early on.

I once befriended a new client who had just been hired. I helped her get up to speed on her job, helped her look good in front of her boss, and helped her understand what the person who had her job before her did right and wrong. In the beginning it was terrific, and I looked forward to my conversations with her. In a day full of rejection, calling her was an absolute delight. Then after six months she got promoted and was not in any way involved in buying my products.

New people can be needy. If you are in a position to really help them, you can spend lots and lots of time doing it. Sometimes I get sucked into spending far more time than I can possibly justify; although it's good to look long-term at the potential this person can return to you, it is easy to spend too much time servicing a client whose ultimate value to you is unpredictable. When a company makes a new hire or promotes someone into a new position, there is a period of evaluation that lasts about six months. Very often the company decides whether it made the right decision or not. It's easy to end up helping people who get promoted, transferred, or fired relatively quickly. It's a time management challenge that has to be evaluated case by case.

Selling Strategies

1. Initially sell on price.

I find that incompetent clients are more impressed by price than they should be. Typically it takes time and experience to understand how to buy the best value in a market. But if there is no experience, buying ramps down to the lowest common denominator, and in any buying process the lowest common denominator is price. Price is the easiest to understand, and buying on price is the easiest to justify. If you are in a position to offer initial low rates, it will often make the sale to the incompetent client in the quickest way possible. The problem is that sales made solely on price tend not to stay in place. You offer a lower price and your client gives you the business, but unless there is some additional value associated with the sale, your sale will be gone the next time a competitor goes in and offers a similar product for 50 cents less. For more information on dealing with incompetent clients who are buying on price alone, see Chapter 1.

2. Give the client a "better way" presentation.

What you would really like to do with an incompetent client is sit him down, grab him by the lapels, shake him, explain to him that he is incompetent, and completely redirect him. Dream on! You are the salesperson and he is the client, and as they say, "The client is always right." Instead, do your best Dale Carnegie act and put the whole thing in positive terms. Give him a presentation that shows him point by point how buying from you presents specific measurable benefits. By presenting your product in this way, you are also educating your client on how to buy from you without mentioning that this is something that many people in his position already know.

3. Sell on relationships.

Except for inexperienced clients who may develop competence as time goes on, most incompetent clients get and keep their jobs through relationships. I find that people who get and justify their position through relationships are often best sold through them. Put aside the idea that this person should not be in a position to buy from you. This doesn't matter; he has the job and you have to call on him. On some level he knows that he does not have the necessary skills to buy the best value for his company. What many do is to bond with a supplier whom they trust, whom they believe will act in their best interest and look out for them. Make sure that this supplier is you. Take the high road and desperately try to win their trust above all. For more ideas, see Chapter 11.

4. Explain how to buy from you.

A client who is incompetent in terms of evaluating products is likely to be incompetent in terms of dealing with a professional buying situation. Sometimes he will innocently ask you for things he should not expect. Sometimes he does not know how to ask for things he is entitled to. I often will do an unscheduled side coaching session, where I give him a crash course in how to be a better buyer. I start by explaining the opportunities he is missing, and if appropriate, I segue into some of the things that he is asking for that may be a little out of line. I do this little coaching session as unnoticeably as possible. It is not a part of the anticipated discussion of our sales call, I do not mention it in my follow-up letter, and I do not bring it up again. It is like our little secret meeting where I give him the facts of life about how to buy. Most clients in this position are extremely grateful, and I find that if they are more educated buyers, they tend to buy from me more often.

5. Help get the client permission to buy.

Incompetent clients are typically getting direction from someone else in the organization. They are often given the budget to spend, but have to get approval for every purchase. Many incompetent clients run scared most of the time. Even if they have the money, they have to get permission to buy. If you can find out what kind of permission your client needs to get and from whom, you can often be more effective. For one client of mine, it meant breaking down any purchase into increments that were under $2,000. Once we broke purchases down into parcels like that, the sales went through much more smoothly. Another client needed his superior's approval to sign off on any purchase. His superior traveled constantly. By arranging for a group meeting with his superior and the person I called on, where he preapproved several of these purchases at a time, we were able to grease the skids for several purchases in a row.

6. Use momentum.

Many incompetent people are running scared so much of the time that they are afraid to rock the boat for any kind of purchase. If you currently have their business, you are in the strongest possible position. Going back for reorders tends to be easy when the client you have is afraid to rock the boat with a new supplier. The trick, of course, is to get him to start being your customer in the first place, but as you are contemplating how to get him started, consider that incompetent clients very often like the comfort and security of buying over and over again from the same supplier.

7. Evaluate him for time investment.

Client incompetence represents an incredible opportunity to
control accounts like few others. The key is to objectively evaluate the future success of this client as an individual and as
a selling opportunity. Although every client is in his or her
own individual situation, here are some general thoughts on investing time in a variety of different kinds of incompetent
clients.

a. *Lazy clients.* I love lazy clients; they are unambitious
people who really don't care whom they buy from, but they will
buy from you if you provide for them a path of least resistance.
When I called on one client he told me he had so much to do
that he was planning on "taking his work home" that afternoon.
Later on the same morning call, he started fishing around to see
whether he could get an invitation to lunch. Lazy clients can be
a good investment. If you can develop a relationship where you
do some of their work, very often you can end up with a disproportionately high percentage of their business. I have one lazy
client whom every year I help write his buying plan, help write
his internal memos justifying his proposals (including the one
for my product), and provide strategic information to help win
his political fights. I don't mind the extra work since it means
more business for me. He knows that if he places his business
with me, I will help him get his job done. It's a relationship that
works well for both of us.

b. *Political appointments.* Most of these people are not worth
much investment, since very often they are caretakers who only
appear to be controlling the buying. They often require a lot of
attention and hand-holding, and very often the buying influence
is elsewhere. They can be very tricky to handle, since most political appointments are extremely defensive about their turf. This
makes it very hard to go over their heads, even though there are
times when it seems the logical thing to do.

c. *Clients appointed through nepotism.* Nepotism is often a terrific investment. First off, don't jump to conclusions. I know
the president of a small manufacturer of very unglamourous
transmission equipment who is the grandson of the company's

founder. Compared with other people in his position, he is a clear cut above them. Had it not been for his involvement in his family's business, it is likely that this bright, progressive professional would have been attracted to a different business entirely. Here, nepotism worked in the company's favor by attracting a far more capable person to the position than could normally be found on the open market. But more often it goes the other way. I have called on the daughter of a company's founder, the son of another division head, a mistress of a high-level company executive, a cousin of the owner who was a drunk, all of whom were hopelessly incompetent. These people could not make a living on their own and had to fall back on their family's generosity. But nepotism among incompetents can still work for you. I once discovered the son of a company president working in a low-level position where I would call on him. Since he was living at home at the time, he was like a lightning rod into the company's highest office. After a while a strange thing started to happen. I would pitch an idea to my contact, and suddenly I would hear that the top people in the company were all talking about it. Nepotistic appointments are often viewed internally as information gatherers or even company spies. Their feedback gets listened to at the highest level. Your client may not know anything about buying your product, but he may help get your selling message into the top offices in the company. I say that is worth some investment.

d. *Clients new to the job.* Bright newcomers are worth investment since they do not stay beginners for long. Aggressively servicing beginners is a terrific way to build a relationship at a time when they welcome your input. Consider that farther down the line—after they have formulated their own views, opinions, and experiences—they will not rely on your advice quite so heavily. My favorite thing to do with a newcomer is to give him a "welcome to the job" presentation. Here I walk him through what his predecessors did right and what people in similar positions do to be effective. I also take the time to go over a lot of the basics of how to buy a product like the one I am representing. To really sell a newcomer, it helps to be the first person in the door that they meet with. If you can be their helper first before any of your competitors do the same, it works best. If you are patient and become a helper, you can make a long-term friend who will buy from you for a long time. The other nice thing about calling on newcomers is that they often have a deeper, more intense curiosity than people who have been at this for a while. Very often, since all this is new to them, they come up with new and interesting ways to look at things that help you grow with your job as well.

8. *Be careful about going over his head.*

A cautionary tale: I was once calling on a clearly incompetent client. Through careful planning I met her boss at an international conference where her boss and I were present. We were out of the country far away and she was not there. It seemed like the perfect way to go over her head. Her boss was a terrific guy and we hit it off immediately. The problem was that her boss turned out to be a complete incompetent as well. Very often incompetent clients have incompetent bosses. Going over their heads has no impact except for possibly making them all angry. Before you go over an incompetent client's head, check to see whether there is a "there" there.

Closing Strategies

1. *Ask yourself, "Do I have to make up his mind for him?"*

Here again, very often the technique closing approaches that are written about in many popular books on selling really are effective. All the different ways to ask whether you want a red one or a blue one, which most competent clients these days decry as being manipulative and obvious, are often very appropriate to use when dealing with incompetent clients.

2. *Exploit fear and greed.*

Since most incompetent clients run scared frequently, they will react if they feel that missing an opportunity will make them look bad. You might consider presenting the selling opportunity in terms of it being something that smart buyers are snapping up like crazy and inept buyers will miss out on. Not wanting to identify with the latter is often a motivating factor.

3. Exploit competitive paranoia.

Incompetent clients are often terrified of being outflanked in a competitive buying environment, and are always trying to look good in front of their boss. Getting one up on the competition is one way they may seek to do this.

4. Ask yourself, "Is this really the person I have to sell?"

As I have mentioned, many organizations know that the people they have hired are incompetent in at least some of the responsibilities they have to execute. If you think your client has no real buying authority, refer to Chapter 4.

20

The Client Who
Does Not Like Your
Company

From the Tough Calls survey:

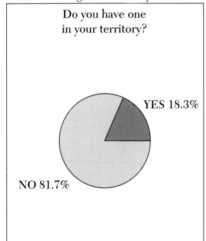

Do you have one
in your territory?

YES 18.3%

NO 81.7%

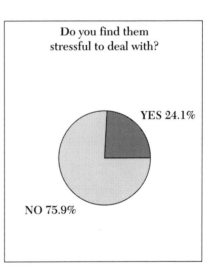

Do you find them
stressful to deal with?

YES 24.1%

NO 75.9%

"Perception is harder to change than reality."
Sales Manager, automatic transmissions, Indianapolis, Ind.

Your clients are paid to look critically at the products or services that they buy from you. One of the things that they need to evaluate is your company, that is, the company that creates and markets the products you are selling. If you work for a large company, there are probably people working in the marketing department who are very concerned with your company's image in the market you sell to. If your client has a negative perception of your company, it is going to count against you. It can prevent you from making an initial sale or can act like a cancer that slowly eats away at your relationship with an existing one. Somehow your client just gets the idea that your company is not a good place to send her business. Any attitude problem like this exists for a reason. Sometimes I encounter reasons that reflect honest weaknesses in the organization I represent, but far more often it is the result of perceptions created by not managing the company's image in the marketplace. It can be benign neglect or sometimes the result of smears by competitors. Your first job is to find out where the negative perception is coming from. Sometimes clients cannot directly express why they don't like your company; it may just be a feeling that has built up over the years, long before you arrived for your call.

Pitfalls

1. Joining your client in griping about your company.

This can be tempting: You are frustrated with an inefficiency at the home office. It drives you crazy when the complaints from your clients pile up about things that are not your fault and that you have no control over. Your client is frustrated and you're frustrated. They start griping . . . but you really can't join them, you have to be a sales professional and rise above this to represent your company. Express concern to your client, get feedback from her, and send it to the home office in the hopes that whatever problems are going on there can be corrected. Thank your client for the feedback and tell her that it will help improve the situation in the future. Don't join the gripe session. If you are both in agreement that the company you work for is in a state of confusion, you simply will have a harder time selling her the next order.

2. Defending your company as being perfect.

In order to be influential while representing your company, you cannot come off like a monochromatic yes man. The most influential salespeople I know are ones who come off as real people and who build credibility to the point where they can influence their clients. If your company has an honest weakness and your client knows about it, you are not going to make points by denying it. Instead, try to minimize the shortcomings. If your company does not have as wide a product line as a competitor, sell your client on the idea that by limiting the number of different products, you are able to maintain higher levels of quality because you are focused on fewer items. Then go on and ask what difference it really makes for her business to carry a lot of models that she really doesn't use. Flat-out denial hurts your credibility, but by acknowledging then minimizing your company's weaknesses you build a sense of honesty that will make you more influential on the account.

3. *Thinking your company has a worse reputation than it actually does.*

In sales you typically hear about the things that go wrong more loudly than the things that go right. Overbearing and demanding problem clients will always be telling you that your home office is out of touch when they do not get the concessions they demand. Over time you will typically hear a lot more negative than positive about the goings-on at the home office. You have to put this in perspective. If you start getting into a funk, call some of your best clients for feedback to counterbalance the negative. Just ask, "How are we doing for you?"

Selling Strategies

1. *Build a positive "buzz."*

In any business category at any given time there are companies that are hot and ones that are not. For some clients, this "not being the hot company" can really count against you. I was once on a sales call in California where a client came out and said, "Hey, what can I say, I'm plugged into what's happening in this business and I know that you are not the hot place to buy right now." Kooky? Maybe, but he articulated the essence of the problem. Yet these kinds of client feelings are more often not expressed as directly as my client did here, but are just as lethal. More typically you hear about some of the smart things your competition might be doing while the client just seems less excited about what you have to say.

Building a buzz is selling the idea that your company is in fact the hot company to be dealing with. Selling a buzz is more subtle than a direct sales pitch for your company. A buzz does not come from what you say about your company; it comes from what other people say about your company. The way you can build a buzz is to tap into second-party information about your product or company that is positive. The beauty of building a buzz is that it need not be a scientific sample or a comprehensive survey of what's really going on; it's just *incremental* evidence gathered from here and there that seems to point to a trend. Here are several ways to build a buzz:

a. *Ask your best clients for testimonials that you can use on other sales calls*. They need not be elaborate. If a client says something positive about your company on a call, simply ask her whether she can put that statement down in a simple letter on her company's letterhead.

b. *Check financial reports about your company*. If your company is publicly traded, there will be information about it somewhere. Financial reports go up and down. When they tick upward, share the information with your clients.

c. *Do an article search*. If you live in a major city, there is probably a business library where you can go to do an article search about your company. You can also use online services like CompuServe and America Online, where this kind of search can be very inexpensive and take only minutes.

d. *Print out a chat room conversation from an on-line service*. I once secured a sale by plugging into a CompuServe professional chat room and printing out a few actual entries for a product made by a company that I was trying to sell to. Some of the comments indicated that these people would be very interested in a product like the one I was selling. When I shared these comments from cyberspace with my client, it helped to build the buzz.

2. Become your whole company.

Most of your clients will never visit your home office, and many more will never meet anyone from your home office face to face. If the only face-to-face contact your client has with your company is you, then perceptually you can become the whole company. As appropriate, take more charge of the account. Tell your client that you will handle certain details personally that might otherwise be handled by people at the home office. Instead of having smaller service matters handled by phone, fax, or mail, tell her to send them all to you so that you can take care of them personally. Handling these little details may be a time drain, but it will give you higher visibility on the account, and slowly they will stop thinking about calling your company and start calling you when there is a problem. I remember Joe, a now retired salesperson, who would explain a competitive selling situation in this way: "It's simple," Joe would say, "the client bought from only two companies, Joe's company and Jim's company."

3. Take someone from the home office on a road trip.

This may be part of your routine anyway, but having a visit from the home office is a way to say, "We care, we want to meet you." If you are in a situation where this statement really needs to be made, titles can be very important. The best title for someone from the home office who comes out with you is that of someone who is involved in the shaping of the actual product that you are selling. Here, the psychology of the call becomes one where the home office comes out to listen to an important client to help shape the future of the product. Clients love this. It's flattering, it's engaging, and it really shows interest in their feedback on a substantive level. The worst title for someone to bring on a road trip is anyone in sales management. Often the psychology of these kinds of trips points to the idea that the home office is checking up on the salesperson.

4. Give a corporate presentation.

For some clients, taking the time to put a face on your company is an indirect but effective way to ultimately make a sale. In our headlong rush to meet quotas and close orders it is easy to forget that the company you sell for could be part of your selling presentation. Major corporations spend millions of dollars on image advertising, and you can make this a part of your next presentation. The challenge is to say something meaningful. Most corporations these days have corporate philosophies that include statements that, if put side by side, would sound quite similar. They tend to include a statement about high customer satisfaction, product quality, and industry leadership. Mentioning these may be academically correct but not terribly interesting for your client. If you can find a way to relate these same concepts to your client's business, you can make much bigger points. Describe leadership by talking about technologies, policies, or practices that your company has actually pioneered. Describe customer satisfaction by mentioning a few of your satisfied customers, specifically why they are satisfied, and how they are being handled that makes their situation unique. This is all a lot easier to describe than it is to do, but somehow the details of your company's activity always contain some interesting items that relate to your customer's business. Whenever I make a corporate presentation, I always get someone commenting, "Oh, I didn't know that about your company," at some point in the presentation.

5. Grant an unexpected goodwill concession.

Sometimes in the give-and-take of an ongoing client-seller relationship, it is easy to forget to take a step back and remember who is doing the buying and who is doing the selling. If you have come through a tough period where there have been a lot of back-and-forth negotiations or concessions granted for mixups, it may be time to just take a step back and assess the buyer-seller relationship and how it is going. Does it seem like a romance, or do both parties (including you) feel that they're getting the short end of the stick? Sometimes you have to do something just to say "thank you." Words are a start, but they never seem to be nearly as meaningful as some kind of concession. The concession may not necessarily be large or costly, but if it is granted unexpectedly, sometimes it makes big points. When you grant a goodwill concession, you really should make a big to-do out of it, since the only real benefit of doing it is to get a sense of goodwill, so you might take time to make sure you get your money's worth. Let your client know what you are going to do and why, then grant the concession.

6. Get the client to know someone from the home office personally.

Depending on the kind of product you sell, there may be someone in your home office who is in a service capacity who can be stepped up to be more of a client contact person. If you can arrange for a face-to-face meeting at an industry function, or just give them both biographical details of each other, sometimes you can foster a relationship. Get them started talking and encourage your service person to give you regular feedback.

7. Find out why.

Sometimes bad feelings about your company are more than just a perception. Sometime there is a real reason why the client doesn't like your company. If you think there is a negative perception of your company, just ask, "Why?" I find most often that the best way to do this is in a face-to-face meeting. Here are some possible ways to counter several specific situations.

a. *The client had a bad previous experience.* This is the hardest negative to overcome. If you have lost business that you once had, getting it back is rough. If there was a customer service problem or a problem with the product, go into the details of the problem and specifically point out how things have been improved in substantive ways and how this would likely never happen again. Of course the problem is that companies, like nature, abhor a vacuum, and if you have lost your client's business it is likely that your client has replaced buying from you with buying from a competitor. The toughest business to get back is business that you have lost.

b. *The salesperson the client dealt with before you was an idiot.* I have had to deal with this several times. For most of your clients, just showing up will make the difference. Your very presence says, "OK, I'm not a jerk and the person who was in my territory before me is really gone, so let's get on with it." But for your more skeptical clients there is a second perception barrier to cross. It's possible that they think you are the fluke and that the home office that hired your predecessor is still out of touch with reality. Once when I was in this situation, going on the road with my sales manager and having him personally apologize for the behavior of my predecessor did the trick. Sometimes a little groveling from the home office goes a long way.

c. *You have been smeared by a direct competitor.* I love it when this happens. If your competitor has manipulated the facts to make you look bad, he has handed you a loaded gun. First, say thank you, since the fact that your competitor would go so far out of his way to smear you shows that he is taking you very seriously. Second, gather the facts of the attack and document everything. Third, document the case for your rebuttal. Call your client and request time to clear your good name. Sometimes even clients who don't like to meet with you too often like the human drama of having one supplier defend herself against the attack of another. Go on the call and present your competitor's attack and your case against it. As your client realizes just how desperate your competition must be to manipulate things in these ways, you spin a negative perception about your competitor and build credibility for yourself.

d. *Your client has made an emotional decision not to buy from you.* This is very common. Your client has a long-standing relationship with a competitor and as a result does not really want to do business with you. Through persistence you get the appointment and personally make a compelling case for your product. Sometimes talking about your company is the only way out. Your client might say, "Well, I like what you say about your product and I think I can do business with you personally, but I've heard some awful things about people who have had business relationships with your company in the past." This may not be the client's real perception; it may just be an objection thrown out to buy some time. It may be that this client is just having a difficult time emotionally adjusting to the idea of doing business with you. If you persistently keep trying to sell her, you'll get this client eventually.

e. *The client has heard bad news from Wall Street.* "I hear your stock took a dive"; "I hear your company is laying off a lot of people." Talk to your manager to find out what the news really means and how you might counter the negative marketplace perception this kind of news might create. If your stock has taken a five-point drop, you may point out that this is only a small percentage of its actual value. If people have been laid off, you might point out how this is not uncommon these days and it will make for a more competitive company in the future. Whatever the details are, if you talk with your management you will find a way to put a more positive spin on the bad news. If all this fails, point out that business publications like the *Wall Street Journal* and *Fortune* are full of turnaround stories where companies that fell behind quickly turned things around, regained momentum, and got back on top. Down does not mean down forever. Sometimes it's just the natural up-and-down pattern that many companies take as they move through their business life.

f. *A problem that was "solved" before was not really solved.* I once had a client, a good client, who suddenly stopped buying from me. Despite several telephone conversations, I simply could not get a reason out of him why he was not buying from me. Finally, I secured a face-to-face visit. We entered his office, both sat down and exchanged pleasantries. Before I could shift into the more substantive side of the presentation that I had planned for him, he let me have it. Two years ago there had been a small error made on an order that he had placed, and we granted a small concession as compensation. Evidently it satisfied him, but months later when his boss found out about it, he was furious. The client was too embarrassed to bring this up with me since he had long ago told me that the problem was behind us. Unfortunately, the problem surfaced again and his boss was putting a lot of pressure on him to find different suppliers. Once I knew what the problem was, it was not hard to solve, but sometimes problems that you thought were resolved come back like a bad penny. If you sense that this might be happening with your client, sometimes it makes sense just to ask, "Are we having any problems that I don't know about?"

8. Ask yourself, "Is it because we are the market leader?"

If your company is the leader in the market you sell to, expect that people are going to be taking potshots at you. Typical labels include "arrogant," "insensitive," and "too big for their britches." There is a natural tendency in any market for the leading products in a category to carry with them a price premium based on some kind of performance advantage or perceived prestige. Competitors or clients who do not want to meet the premium pricing may fall by the wayside and shout, "Arrogant!" If you are getting this kind of feedback and believe that your products are priced fairly for the value they deliver, simply ignore the feedback. It's just part of the price of leadership.

9. Ask yourself, "Is it about concessions?"

In a hardball price negotiation you will typically be pushed beyond the point where you have the authority to make concessions. Ultimately, the home office will decide just how far these concessions can go before they're stopped. Hardball negotiators know this, and so the home office becomes a psychological target. Hearing from hardball negotiators that the home office is out of touch with reality is routine and should be expected from them. Humor them and ignore the comments; this is not a real objection, but just an ongoing behavior you have to put up with. For ideas on dealing with this situation, see Chapter 6.

Closing Strategies

1. Offer a "screw-up guarantee."

If your company has the reputation of being a bad place to do business because it screws things up, tell your client that you will offer her a guarantee where significant concessions will be granted if the specific kinds of mistakes that your client is expecting get made. Typically, these kinds of negative perceptions are exaggerated and it is unlikely that your company will make these mistakes. Very often offering a "screw-up guarantee" means getting new business or increasing old business. I find that sales managers are amenable to these kinds of agreements.

2. *Close him on the product you are selling.*

Mention your company as little as possible. If you get any resistance, say, "Look, this is the product you want, and I will see that it works for you. Can I have the order?"

3. *If you get past the negative perception of your company, using any of the selling strategies mentioned before you can go on to close this client like any other client.*

21
You Are Not Alone

Dealing with problem clients is not about just strategies and tactics. A lot of it also has to do with how you feel after having dealt with them. Whenever I get hit with a serious problem client situation the first question I ask is: "Why me?" After trying to find ways to cope with the situation, the next three questions are: "Does anyone else have to deal with this?" "Does anyone else find this as stressful to deal with as I do?" and finally, "Why do these people act the way they do?" I conducted a national survey for this book, and now I have some answers. It is my hope that by comparing your personal experiences with this national sample, you will come away with a better understanding of just where you stand.

Finding 1: One out of every six clients in America is considered by the people who call on them to be a problem client.

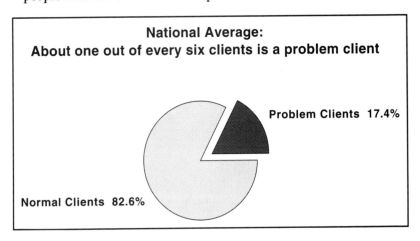

National Average:
About one out of every six clients is a problem client

Problem Clients 17.4%

Normal Clients 82.6%

Finding 2: The most common problem client by far is the client who grinds you on price. Three quarters of all sales territories report having at least one. If you don't have a price grinder in your territory now, get ready, odds are you will someday.

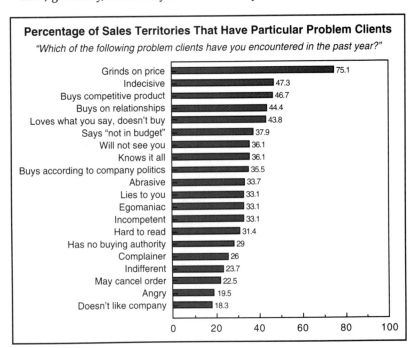

Percentage of Sales Territories That Have Particular Problem Clients

"Which of the following problem clients have you encountered in the past year?"

Grinds on price	75.1
Indecisive	47.3
Buys competitive product	46.7
Buys on relationships	44.4
Loves what you say, doesn't buy	43.8
Says "not in budget"	37.9
Will not see you	36.1
Knows it all	36.1
Buys according to company politics	35.5
Abrasive	33.7
Lies to you	33.1
Egomaniac	33.1
Incompetent	33.1
Hard to read	31.4
Has no buying authority	29
Complainer	26
Indifferent	23.7
May cancel order	22.5
Angry	19.5
Doesn't like company	18.3

0   20   40   60   80   100

Finding 3: The percentage of your clients who are problem clients depends on what you sell. People who sell services have a higher percent of problem clients than people who sell a physical product. People who sell financial products have an extremely high percentage of problem clients, about one in five.

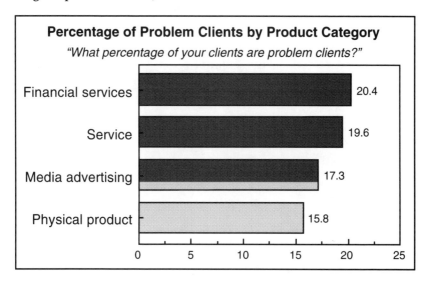

Percentage of Problem Clients by Product Category

"What percentage of your clients are problem clients?"

Financial services	20.4
Service	19.6
Media advertising	17.3
Physical product	15.8

Finding 4: The kinds of problem clients whom you encounter also vary according to what you sell. The price grinder is the most common problem client, but not for people who sell financial services, whose top problem is the indecisive client. Since it is easier to make side-by-side comparisons with physical products, people who sell them tend to encounter problematic behavior deriving from comparison shopping. People who sell services deal more with difficulties in getting decisions and commitments made. Media/advertising salespeople face similar problems as do those selling a service. Presented here are the top five problem clients for these different product groups:

Service	Physical Product	Media/Advertising	Financial Product
1. Grinds you on price	1. Grinds you on price	1. Grinds you on price	1. Is indecisive
2. Is indecisive	2. Buys elswhere: likes a competitive product	2. Says, "It's not in the budget"	2. Buys elswhere on relationships
3. Loves what you say, then does not buy	3. Buys elsewhere on relationships	3. Buys elswhere: likes a competitive product	3. Grinds you on price
4. Says, "It's not in the budget"	4. Is indecisive	4. Loves what you say, then does not buy	4. Buys elswhere: likes a competitive product
5. Buys elswhere because of company politics	5. Is abrasive	5. Is indecisive	5. Loves what you say, then does not buy

Finding 5: The percentage of your clients who are problem clients depends on your selling style. Salespeople who use a consultative style of selling perceive that they have a higher number of problem clients in their territories, more than one in five. People with a "closer" selling style perceive that they have a much lower number of problem clients, only about one in ten.

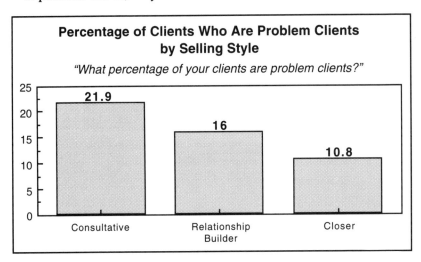

Finding 6: People who sell mainly to Fortune 500 corporations encounter about twice the number of problem clients as people who do not. I isolated two samples for comparison, one with people who get little or no business from Fortune 500 corporations (20% or less). The second sample was from people who get the vast majority of their business from Fortune 500 corporations (70% or more).

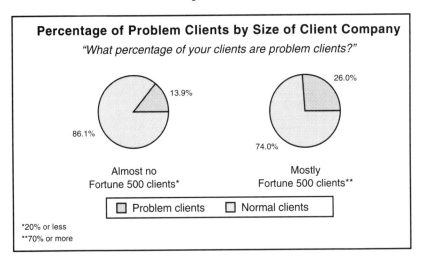

Finding 7: Salespeople who call on Fortune 500 corporations are twice as likely to encounter egomaniacs and abrasive clients. They are also almost three times as likely to encounter incompetent clients. The good news is they are much less likely to have their order canceled when calling on Fortune 500 corporations. Here is a list of the contrasting problem client frequencies:

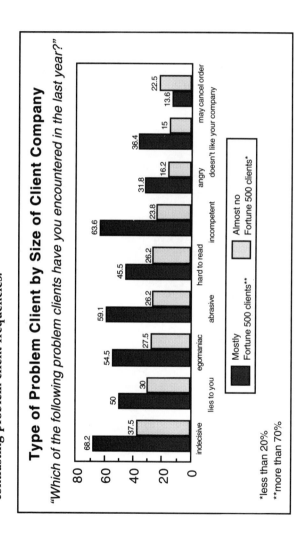

Type of Problem Client by Size of Client Company

"Which of the following problem clients have you encountered in the last year?"

*less than 20%
**more than 70%

Finding 8: Problem clients account for about a third of all job-related stress among salespeople and professionals with client contact responsibilities.

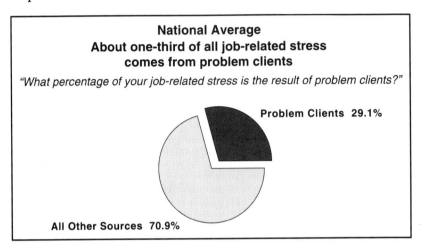

National Average
About one-third of all job-related stress
comes from problem clients

"What percentage of your job-related stress is the result of problem clients?"

Problem Clients 29.1%

All Other Sources 70.9%

Finding 9: Problem clients who affect you on a more personal level are the most stressful to deal with. While the price grinder may be the most common problem client by far, he or she is only the sixth most stressful to deal with. This is probably because they are so common that most people in a client contact position have learned to deal with them.

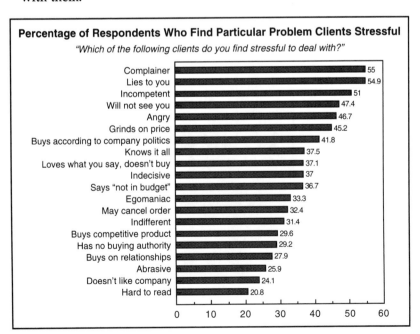

Percentage of Respondents Who Find Particular Problem Clients Stressful

"Which of the following clients do you find stressful to deal with?"

Client	Percentage
Complainer	55
Lies to you	54.9
Incompetent	51
Will not see you	47.4
Angry	46.7
Grinds on price	45.2
Buys according to company politics	41.8
Knows it all	37.5
Loves what you say, doesn't buy	37.1
Indecisive	37
Says "not in budget"	36.7
Egomaniac	33.3
May cancel order	32.4
Indifferent	31.4
Buys competitive product	29.6
Has no buying authority	29.2
Buys on relationships	27.9
Abrasive	25.9
Doesn't like company	24.1
Hard to read	20.8

Finding 10: Men and women find different problem clients stressful to deal with. Here are the top five stress-causing problem clients for both men and women. Two of the five were identical but while women find complainers and clients who buy elsewhere due to company politics to be the most stressful, men find liars and incompetents the most stressful.

The five most stressful clients to deal with for men and women:

Men	Women
1. Lies to you	1. Complains about everything
2. Is incompetent	2. Buys elswhere due to company politics
3. Grinds you on price	3. Will not see you
4. Will not see you	4. Says, "It's not in the budget"
5. Gets angry	5. Gets angry

Finding 11: Experienced salespeople report a greater percentage of job-related stress from problem clients than beginners do. There are many aspects of a salesperson's job that become less stressful with experience. However, stress from dealing with problem clients does not diminish.

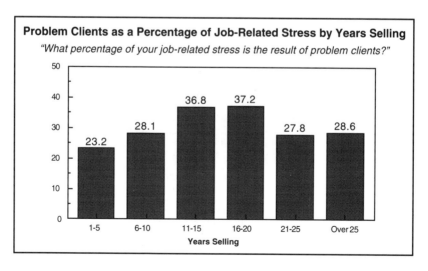

Problem Clients as a Percentage of Job-Related Stress by Years Selling

"What percentage of your job-related stress is the result of problem clients?"

Finding 12: Insecurity motivates clients to act in problematical ways more than anything else according to the people who call on them. A buyer who is insecure and afraid of losing her job will display a lot of problematic behavior.

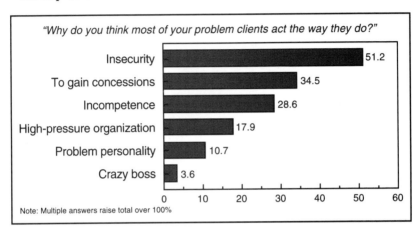

"Why do you think most of your problem clients act the way they do?"

Insecurity	51.2
To gain concessions	34.5
Incompetence	28.6
High-pressure organization	17.9
Problem personality	10.7
Crazy boss	3.6

Note: Multiple answers raise total over 100%

Finding 13: Women believe that client insecurity motivates problem clients much more than men do. Men are almost three times as likely to think that problem client's behaviors are caused by incompetence.

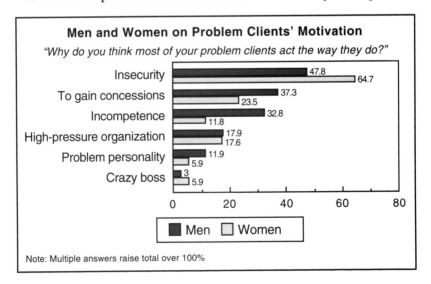

Men and Women on Problem Clients' Motivation

"Why do you think most of your problem clients act the way they do?"

	Men	Women
Insecurity	47.8	64.7
To gain concessions	37.3	23.5
Incompetence	32.8	11.8
High-pressure organization	17.9	17.6
Problem personality	11.9	5.9
Crazy boss	3	5.9

■ Men □ Women

Note: Multiple answers raise total over 100%

Finding 14: People who work for very small companies (1 to 5 employees) find more problem client behavior motivated by client insecurity than do those who work for any other size of company.

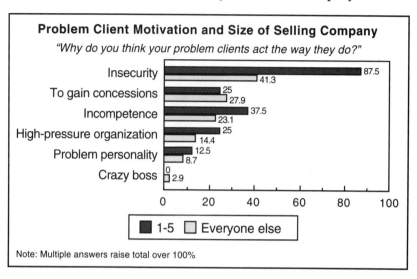

Finding 15: More than one-fourth of the time a sales manager spends talking with salespeople about clients is spent talking about problem clients.

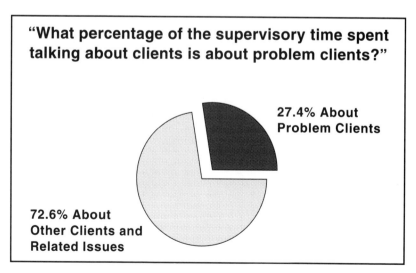

Finding 16: Problem clients can be good for business. Salespeople who work for companies that experienced a big increase in business over the previous year report having the highest percentage of problem clients. Companies whose sales were flat over the previous year report the least number of problem clients.

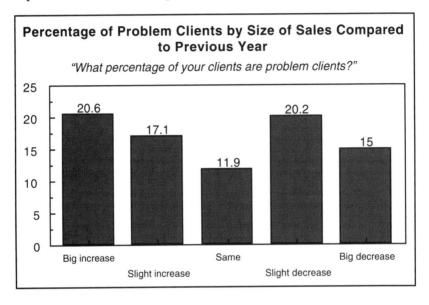

Percentage of Problem Clients by Size of Sales Compared to Previous Year

"What percentage of your clients are problem clients?"

Parting Words

"Problem clients usually turn into your strongest customers."
Advertising salesman, New York, N.Y.

Problem clients: Love them or hate them, they are the reason we are here. If every client you had just handed you an order without a fight, we salespeople and client contact professionals would soon be unemployed.

But problem clients are more than a reason for justifying our jobs, they represent an opportunity. As I have left selling positions and looked back, I found that the strongest relationships I made, the best customers I had, all started as problem clients. The best clients you have are those to whom you have had to prove your value and that of your products. A sales territory without problem clients is a territory without opportunity.

Index